For R
In Memory

TALES OF
OLD OCKINGTON

**Re-living 2,000 Years
in Okehampton – A Dartmoor Community**

Copyright © 2002 Alan Endacott MA AMA

Published by Orchard Publications
2 Orchard Close, Chudleigh, Devon TQ13 0LR
Telephone 01626 852714

ISBN 1 898964 51 3

All rights reserved. No part of this publication may be reproduced, stored in a retrieval system, or transmitted in any form or by any means, without the permission of the copyright holder.

Printed by
Hedgerow Print
Crediton EX17 1ES

CONTENTS

Acknowledgements		iii
Introduction		iv
Chapter 1.	Following the Eagle	1
Chapter 2.	A forgotten Age of Princes, Kings and Saints	8
Chapter 3.	At the Crossroads	13
Chapter 4.	A New Town is Born	17
Chapter 5.	A Common Bond	23
Chapter 6.	Plague, Bloodshed and Change	39
Chapter 7.	Chronicles of a Turbulent Time	50
Chapter 8.	The Commonwealth and Beyond	65
Chapter 9.	When Squire Ruled All	76
Chapter 10.	Reform, Education and Improvement	87
Chapter 11.	Edwardian Dreams	100
Chapter 12.	Into the Modern Age	113
Notes		123
Bibliography		128
Index		131

ACKNOWLEDGEMENTS

I would like to thank the following for their assistance: I am indebted to my successor, Maurie Webber, at the Museum of Dartmoor Life for allowing access to its archive and library and especially to Paul Hamblyn for his assistance in checking facts and testing hypotheses! Dr. R. L. Taverner was always a great inspiration, with his in-depth knowledge of medieval and Civil War Okehampton, but, sadly, he passed away during the preparation of this book. I am grateful to Jacquie Woods of the Celtic Village, Chacewater (near Truro) for her advice and allowing me to photograph the reconstructed houses there and to Diane Herrod for her assistance with proof-reading and editing. Thanks are also due to the Museum of Dartmoor Life and Okehampton Town Council and English Heritage for allowing the reproduction of illustrations and reconstructions and to Julie Routley for assistance in preparing photographs and illustrations. Then there are the countless individuals who I had the privilege of meeting during my time at the Museum and Finch Foundry and who have contributed unwittingly through their reminiscences of life in and around 'Okey'. However, this publication might not have come about at all had it not been for the support and encouragement of a few people – particularly Rose Young and her late husband, John, my parents and of course my family for their forbearance as I 'burnt the midnight oil' over two years to complete the task. Now it is done and I thank you for reading it.

INTRODUCTION

Have you ever wondered what life was like in your local town or village one hundred, one thousand or even two thousand years ago? Was there even a settlement there then? How would it have appeared and what would everyday life have been like for the inhabitants? What sort of relationships would they have had with each other? How would they have made their living – or even survived such hard conditions?

If you have ever pondered on such things then this is the book for you. It is actually based on the medieval market town of Okehampton – *Ockington* or *Okey* in the local vernacular – on the northern tip of Dartmoor, but it could be about practically any inland town in Devon or East Cornwall. With the aid of illustrations and chapters giving the historical context, it describes the settlement at different stages of its development over the last two thousand years with the help of various historical characters. The characters chosen are mostly based on real people and their lives have been pieced together from a range of sources – written records, archaeological investigations, architectural studies and anecdotes – glued together with a little healthy conjecture! The individual characters are brought to life on the assumption that, although circumstances and protocols may have changed, basic human nature has not. Please note at this point that the views expressed by the characters don't necessarily reflect those of the author!

Much of the book is based on historical 'fact' – or current interpretations of the written or archaeological evidence. Historical notes at the end give further explanation where this may be helpful to the reader and indicate where conjecture is employed, lest the historical record be unintentionally corrupted. The author readily acknowledges the work of the greater authorities that have provided some of the raw materials for this work through thorough academic research and publication. Recreating the past life of an area can only ever be a 'best guess' and, inevitably, other people's interpretations of the evidence may differ. A full bibliography of sources referred to in its research is available at the end for any one who may wish to delve for themselves and reach their own conclusions.

And, finally, history is a living, evolving thing. No history can ever be 'definitive'. You are part of it today, as we enter a new millennium. It is at the very heart of ancient communities like Okehampton – you never know, you may even feature in a history of the next millennium so, go on and make it, record it, cherish it and, most importantly, enjoy it!

FOLLOWING THE EAGLE

Lucinus Silvanus stood at the top of the hill and surveyed the surrounding countryside. A vast forest stretched mile upon mile to the north, west and east, punctuated by occasional wisps of smoke that gave away the location of the scattered farms of the native Celts. To the south stretched the foothills of Dartmoor, clothed in a dense, low scrub, cleared here and there in an effort to scratch an existence from the thin and often waterlogged soils. Brooding over all stood the rugged peaks of the moor's highest hills, their granite tors etched by ice and wind over countless millennia.

Fifty years had passed since the birth of Christ in a far off land, the story as yet unheard of in these pagan lands. Indeed, Lucinus himself was of Celtic stock and so was not entirely unfamiliar with the religion, language and culture of the local tribe of the Dumnonniians – 'the people of the land'. His own native home land was the Roman province of Argentoratum (*1*), by the forested banks of the Rhine in eastern Gaul but his goal was to obtain Roman citizenship and the great privileges that would bestow on him and his heirs. First he had to finish his twenty-five year stint as an auxiliary infantry soldier in the Roman Army, helping to expand and secure the northern frontiers of the Empire. His regiment marched, fought and worked alongside the Roman citizens who made up the five and a half thousand strong Second Augustan Legion under the command of General Titus Flavius Vespasianus, who was later to become Emperor Vespasian. Their task was to secure the territory of the Dumnonii (modern Devon, Cornwall and western Somerset). Like most men in his position, Lucinus was in two minds about the battles and skirmishes that broke up the monotony and rigid discipline of legionary life. They hadn't met much resistance since establishing the legionary fortress at Isca (Exeter) and he wasn't too sorry to have the tough campaign against the fierce tribe of Durotriges further east behind him.

Since the initial invasion of some seven years before the Legion had successfully fought thirty battles, stormed around twenty hillforts and subdued two tribes. Faced with little coherent or concerted defence from the native British, their discipline and excellent military planning meant that the further conquest of this remote corner of the southwest of Britain was rather less eventful by comparison. In fact it was a source of some disappointment to the officers who lusted after military glory. To be truthful, there was little to interest his Roman masters down here, apart from slaves and the centuries-old tin trade. As there were plentiful supplies of the latter from Spain, even this wasn't a major attraction (*2*). Because of the poor roads, such trade was mostly conducted via trading posts on the coast but his masters didn't want to leave any pockets of resistance inland that might provide the British with an opportunity to re-group and fight back.

By and large the natives here were friendly enough though. The children and younger women in particular greeted the soldiers warmly and excitedly. As an old hand, Lucinus had grown accustomed to the shouting and screaming of bands of children who ran alongside the lines and tried to copy as they marched through their scattered farm settlements. His Celtic origins also made him feel slightly uneasy though when he encountered the taunts of the men (and some formidable women!) who treated the auxiliaries with either suspicion or outright hostility. A particular object of derision was the Roman style outfit they wore, consisting of a tunic and kilt. Like him they had been used to wearing woven woollen trousers for protection against the cold and thick undergrowth. Their warriors bared their chests and painted their bodies with woad to frighten their enemies. No self-respecting Celtic warrior would hide behind armour other than their sturdy round shield that they used more like a weapon. It was no accident that the auxiliaries shared a common heritage with these people. Part of their role was to persuade their fellow Celts of the benefits of aspiring to Roman citizenship and, in doing so, to swell the army's ranks still further. In turn, they would join auxiliaries in other Roman provinces and expand the Empire still further. Perhaps they would be more fortunate and be posted to warmer climes!

The climate in this area had deteriorated over the previous thousand years from the halcyon days of the 'Bronze Age' when the Dumnonians' ancestors had lived and farmed extensively on the higher ground of Dartmoor as well as on the more fertile and well-drained areas of the lowlands. It was now cold and damp for much of the year and the soils generally poor – thin and peaty on the higher ground, waterlogged and clayey on much of the surrounding lowland. Dense forest covered large tracts of the countryside between the moor and the north coast, forming the *mor coed* or 'great wood' (*3*). On the moor, the once cultivated clearings of the farmers of the 'Stone' and 'Bronze' Ages of almost two thousand years before – the period when the great stone temples and places of the dead ancestors were built – had long since grown over. The ancient sacred sites and monuments of 'the ancestors' were still respected and even venerated by their distant descendants and later Celtic immigrants however.

Remains of the round stone houses of the later Bronze Age still abounded on the higher ground where surface building stone was plentiful and were occasionally re-occupied by metal workers and farmers. They provided welcome shelter for those tending flocks or herds on the summer pastures or 'common' lands of the high moor. This seasonal practice had been carried on for a 1000 years already and was just as vital to the 'Iron Age' farming community as good grazing was in short supply due to the need to cultivate the lighter soils of the moor's edge. Land divisions, marked out in the Bronze Age by reaves (low stone banks) to separate common pasturage from tribal lands, were still visible and stretched for long distances around the contours of the higher moor's edge. Parallel reaves; running down at right angles to the contour reaves, that had once divided the tribal lands, could also still be seen. These were often incorporated into the small rectangular fields of later 'Iron Age' farms.

The small farms nestling in the clearings of the great wood also had small fields but the predominant building material was timber rather than stone as it was so plentiful. The pens and fields contained small black cattle, goat-like sheep, pigs, poultry and horses (*4*). The cattle and sheep were kept for their milk and wool as well as providing a source of meat. Horses were eaten too but also served as mounts for Celtic warriors and to pull their war chariots. Along with cattle, they also served as objects of trade and barter as well as contributing towards marriage settlements, as money was not generally in circulation in these parts. Salt was a particularly valued commodity in exchange as it allowed meat to be preserved well into the winter when fodder to keep livestock was scarce.

Cattle, rather than horses, were the beasts of burden and pulled primitive ploughs known as ards. Varieties of wheat, oats and barley were grown to provide flour as well as the ingredients for the barley ale or wheaten beer, flavoured with honey, of which the natives were so fond. It was usually drunk in place of water as this was often contaminated but it did nothing for their temperament or military abilities, other than providing false courage! There was nothing the British warriors liked more than to sit around the fire under the thatched roofed of their chieftain's large round house, feasting and drinking large quantities of ale while boasting of their exploits or telling tales of their heroes and ancestors. Fighting, gambling with dice and field sports such as racing, hurling (a rough ball game) and hunting were all popular pastimes. Wild boar were particularly prized and provided tasty meat for the table.

Ordinary farmers also lived in round houses, not too dissimilar to those built in the district for over a thousand years, only these were built of wattle and daub (woven hazel covered with clay, straw and animal hair) on a timber

Reconstructed Iron Age houses at the Celtic Village, Chacewater, near Truro

Interior of a reconstructed Iron Age house at Worthyvale, Bodmin Moor. Note the vertical loom and central open hearth

structure which also supported the conical thatched roof (5). They were not without their home comforts though – an open hearth for warmth and cooking and a clay oven for baking. Corn was ground on a saddle quern (a hand-held stone ground on a flat stone surface) or a small rotary quern (hand mill). Animal skins and colourful cloth from died wool, woven on a vertical hand loom, provided extra warmth as well as decoration. They used wooden plates and spoons for eating and iron knives or daggers to cut meat. These, along with other iron tools and weapons were made by skilled smiths who also shod horses and made the metal ploughshares that enabled the farmers to tackle the poorer drained soils of the district.

Lucinus was tired after a swift march from the existing six and a half acre (2.5 hectare) fort at Nemetostatio (6) some eight miles (13 km) to the east along the newly laid out road which stretched from hilltop to hilltop in straight stages as determined by the surveyors and scouts who went on ahead. He had spent the past few weeks toiling on its construction with his companions. Although not of the standard of the great Roman highways, such as the Fosse Way to the east of Exeter, its firm foundations, compacted stone surface and drainage ditches were more durable than the brushwood roads sometimes thrown down overnight when in hostile territory in order to surprise the still sleeping enemy. The ability to march large numbers of troops speedily along these roads was one of the keys to their military success. By contrast, the native roads, if you could call them that, were nothing more than dirt tracks linking the isolated farmsteads and the ancient Ridgeway which, though muddy and rough, conveyed much of the trade from far off parts down the spine of the peninsular.

The immediate objective was to secure the territory and continue driving the new road ever westwards and over the Tamar river to link up with friendly coastal trading communities and to mop-up any opposition from the *Cornovii* – 'people of the horn' – along the way. In order to consolidate their position, it was essential that the army established outpost forts at regular intervals along the new military roads. These could be used to fall back on for defence if necessary and as garrisons during the winter months or any break in the campaign. Auxiliaries carried much of the kit required to construct such forts in their packs. A basket, pick, axe, saw and two stakes for the palisade would all help to keep their camp secure until work was progressed on the more permanent defences. In addition to this vital equipment, they had to carry their armour and weapons, a cooking pot and enough grain to last for a couple of weeks – a total weight of 90lbs (40 kg).

It had been decided that a site above the opposite bank of the 'swift and noisy' river – *okement* in the native tongue – would be a suitable place. It lay between the high moor, with its steep sided border valleys and the dense and often marshy woodlands to the north, at a point where the river was still easily forded during most of the year. Their scouts had discovered a small promontory fort, with a single ditch and rampart (bank), overlooking the East Okement where it met the Moor Brook higher upstream. But, in spite of its impressive and lofty position, the fort had not been occupied for generations and the inter-tribal conflicts from which it was born, like those of its larger relations on the north eastern side of Dartmoor, were distant folk memories (*7*). It posed no threat to the new regime and, in any case, their goal lay further west, not south to the, by then, inhospitable wastes of Dartmoor.

After this brief moment of reflection, Lucinus returned to his duties, wondering what lay ahead. He had been sent on ahead with a small contingent and a surveyor to check alignments from a suitable high point. A small signal station had been established on a windswept ridge (Sourton Down) four miles (6.5km) to the west. From here it was possible to communicate by signal fire with units at other high points within a twenty mile (32km) radius. A small fortlet was planned ten miles (16km) to the northwest (Broadbury) on a road to the north coast; another (presumed) was to be built on the far side of the Tamar. The small fort that Lucinus and his comrades were to build was intended to control the crossing of the Okement rivers and the ancient ridge-way that skirted around the northern tip of Dartmoor. The site (*8*) above the east bank, just below the confluence of the two Okement rivers and where it was still fordable, appeared to suit its purpose. Work was to commence without delay, as supplies were limited and the legion's position was vulnerable without forward lines of defence for the main camps and forts to the east.

An area of around two and a half acres (1 hectare) was to be enclosed by a single V shaped ditch and a substantial bank, surmounted by a timber palisade and bearing four timber angle towers at the corners and a gate tower in the centre of each side. The buildings within would also be of timber construction but with clay tiled roofs and would have to be able to accommodate some three hundred and eighty infantry and a hundred and twenty cavalry troops. Lucinus would share a double cubicle in the barracks with five to seven other men. His centurions and decurions (NCOs and officers) would have more spacious accommodation at the ends of the barrack blocks and his commander would have his own house (the *praetorium*) with a dining room (*triclinium*) where he could entertain local chiefs or visiting officers and officials. There would also be a headquarters (*principia*) with a colonnaded front and a central courtyard, stores and granaries, bakehouses and stabling – not to mention the all-important latrines and bathhouses

Of course he had other needs beyond the immediate priorities of food, shelter and security.

His spiritual needs had to be fulfilled – Lucinus looked to the gods to give him strength and courage in battle and to protect his far off family. His gods were drawn from the pantheon of Roman deities, especially Mars, or borrowed from other cultures, such as Mithras, the Persian god of light and wisdom. Portable altars to these gods were carried to wherever the Legion was posted. The priests lay the entrails of sacrificial birds or animals on these in order to predict the future. However, Romans were quite happy to adopt and worship native deities as well and, with his own pagan Celtic roots, a visit to the local shrine of *Nemetona*, 'goddess of the sacred grove' was quite acceptable. A new shrine had been established, on a natural spur of land between the West Okement river and the sacred stream by the grove, in a symbolic gesture of both assimilation and subjugation of the native cult. (*9*)

Naturally, Lucinus and his comrades had material and bodily needs too! It would not be long before a small encampment of artisans, traders and camp followers would become established outside of the gates of the new fort. Only officers were officially allowed to take wives and family with them although many ordinary legionaries did start second families along the route. Such practices were officially frowned upon as not being conducive to good military discipline but they did help to spread the influence of a Romanised way of life to even the most remote corners of the Empire. Lucinus had a wife and children back in Gaul. It had been many months since he had last seen them and he had so much to tell them of his campaign – the battles, people and places encountered along the way and the hardships, boredom and sheer hard work he had endured. He knew it would all prove worthwhile one day. He would go anywhere and do anything to achieve his personal goal by obtaining the ultimate prize of Roman citizenship. Hail Caesar!

A FORGOTTEN AGE OF PRINCES, KINGS AND SAINTS

In more favourable parts of the province, it was not uncommon for old soldiers to set up civilian settlements within the walls of abandoned forts if they had no family to return to or lacked the desire to return to their homelands. Many seized new opportunities in this way and went on to spread Roman civilisation and citizenship to the people of Britain. The far South West did not seem to hold the same attraction though and within twenty years or so of the military occupation, the majority of the soldiers moved on with very few remaining behind to settle. The Second Augustan Legion were called north to assist with the conquest of Wales from a new Legionary fortress in Caerleon while *Isca* (Exeter) went on to become the *Canton* or capital of the *Civitas Dumnoniorum* – the civilian community of Devon and Cornwall – under the protection of its great city walls. The Romanised life-style of the citizens of Isca was very different to that of the families who continued to scratch out an existence on the isolated farmsteads of north Dartmoor though. Life here carried on much the same as before the conquest with gradual inroads being made into the Great Wood. Many of these Iron Age farm sites would continue to be occupied for another two thousand years, others would revert to forest in time, only to be brought back into cultivation centuries later by Saxon settlers. No Roman villas have been discovered in Devon west of Exeter and it seems likely that the traditional round houses, built of perishable materials, remained the norm, thus leaving little trace for modern archaeologists to examine.

The Roman soldiers left their mark never the less, particularly on the minds of the younger generation and the local aristocracy who went on to model their dynasties along Roman lines for many centuries to come and even took up classical studies which helped to keep a rudimentary knowledge of the Latin language alive in the neighbourhood into the early Christian era, as evidenced by a scatter of memorial stones bearing Latin text and Romanised names. Indeed, Dumnonia remained under Roman control for the next three hundred and fifty years. The network of forts established during the first twenty five years of military rule were largely abandoned as the peninsula enjoyed the security and economic benefits of the Roman order. Traders would have introduced Roman customs, technological innovations and goods to many communities on their travels up-and-down the ancient ridgeways and through the coastal ports. An intriguing find of a 'hoard' of around two hundred fourth century coins hidden under a rock near the railway station towards the end of the nineteenth century raises questions as to who left them there and why.

Travellers may also have introduced Christianity to some of the rural pagan population, especially after it became the official religion of the Roman Empire in the year 324 although organised Christian worship appears to have been mainly confined to towns.

With the fall of the Roman Empire in AD 410 the great cities to the east were abandoned one by one or laid bare by the heathen invaders from across the North Sea – Angles, Saxons, Jutes and Frisians. However, it would be many years before they troubled the Western shores of the British Isles. Life in the old province continued much the same for most people. A new aristocracy of petty kings and princes developed in Dumnonia, no doubt modelling themselves on their Roman forebears. We know little about these shadowy figures other than some sketchy contemporary accounts, references in medieval manuscripts recording the lives of the Celtic saints, local folklore and the tantalising archaeological evidence from sites such as Tintagel on the north Cornish coast.

A number of memorial stones, bearing Latin inscriptions or Irish *'ogham script'* characters, can be found dotted around Cornwall, West Devon and the borders of Dartmoor. They record the names some of these otherwise long-forgotten rulers. One such, rather worn, inscription can be seen on a stone cross standing near the modern A30 at Sourton Cross. It may read *'PRINCIP – / IVRIVCI / AVDETI'* – the first word either being a title or, more likely, the Latin name *Principius* and the last is the name *Aude(n)tius.* The stone probably dates from the sixth century but was fashioned into the shape of a rough cross in medieval times. No burial is known to have been associated with it, as in the majority of the examples. A similar stone at Stowford does, however, stand in the oval churchyard, thus indicating a Christian site of great antiquity.

The suffix *stow* – 'a holy place' – appears in several place names in the locality, often in association with the name of the founder of the early Church or Minster on the site . For example St Bridget at Bridestowe and St Petrock at Petrockstowe. Christian missionary saints from Ireland and South Wales were very active at this time, spreading the Gospel to the isolated pagan communities of Devon and Cornwall. Although original dedications to Celtic saints are common in Cornwall, they are much less so in the west of Devon. This doesn't necessarily mean that they were not founded by Celtic missionaries but, rather, that the Christian church in Cornwall tended to remain more conservative and less influenced by later invaders and settlers. It may well be that an early Christian Church was established on the site of the present parish Church of Okehampton but any evidence of a dedication to its founder was either lost or out of favour in 1231 when it was re-consecrated and given the dedication of *All Saints* by Bishop Bronscombe.

The only dark shadow on the horizon during this time of relative peace and prosperity was the ever encroaching frontier of Saxon aggression and settlement from the east. Word must have spread along the old trade routes of the latest incursions and battles. Tales must have been told around the open fires of the chiefs' great round houses, of the exploits of heroes, such as the legendary Arthur, against the heathen foe. The old Celtic warring spirit was re-kindled, long abandoned hillforts re-fortified and the Saxon's western progress was halted for some fifty years. But come they did, slowly and often peacefully at first as pioneer settlers moving into abandoned land but then with fury as raids and skirmishes turned into full blown battles across Dumnonia and the Saxons drove their frontier ever-westwards. In 577 they defeated the Britons at Dyrham (near Bath), thus dividing the Welsh from the *West Welsh* of Dumnonia. In 614 they slaughtered some 2,500 British warriors in a battle at Bindon (near Axmouth), won another at Penselwood in west Somerset in 658 and were fighting at *Posentesbyrig* (possibly Posbury near Crediton) in 661. Then in 682 the West Saxon king Centwine won a decisive victory over the Britons at an unknown location (possibly not too far from Okehampton) and 'drove the Britons in flight as far as the sea'. It is thought that this refers to the Atlantic coast of north west Devon and that the rivers Tamar and Ottery marked the frontier until King Egbert of Wessex finally overran the Britons in 838. Place names provide tangible evidence of this division – those to the west predominantly Cornish, those to the east, mainly Saxon.

Meanwhile the steady migration of people from Dumnonia across the Channel to the Armorican peninsula, which began when the security offered by the Roman Empire was lost, continued apace in the face of the Saxon advance. These people became established in *'Little Britain'* or *Brittany* where the Breton language, very similar to Cornish, still survives. Others moved west of the Tamar or retreated to the poorer lands of Dartmoor and its borders. Once again place names provide evidence of their survival in this area into the Saxon period, for example Wallabrook from *weala* or 'Welshmen' as the Saxons referred to the natives. Many of the Celts who remained behind were taken into slavery by Saxon nobles, while others, such as remote hill farmers, were treated very much as second class citizens judging by their legal standing in matters of compensation or *wergeld* for crimes of murder, assault or theft. Abandoned farms on the more fertile lands provided rich pickings for the incoming settlers. Direct evidence of this kind of inheritance can also be seen place names such as *Yelland* – meaning 'old lands' – just to the west of Okehampton.

There were occasional British raids across the border, for instance in 825 when the Cornish Britons joined forces with the Danes but were defeated at the battle of *Gafolforda* (thought to be Galford in Lewtrenchard parish, 10 miles (16km) to the west of Okehampton) but the Saxon settlers enjoyed more or less unhindered progress as they re-populated the district and established or re-established most of the farms, hamlets and villages we are familiar with today. They also gave many their names. A quick glance at the map will immediately identify them – '-cott' (peasant homestead), '-worthy' (freeman's home), '-ton' (a village or collection of houses). Okehampton itself is first recorded in the early eleventh century in a note in the margin of a missal (service book) of Bishop Leofric of Exeter as *Ocmund tune* or 'Okement ton' – the settlement by the Okement – regarding the freeing of slaves at the cross roads so that they could choose their own destiny.

Precisely when the settlement of Okehampton came into being and what it looked like we will probably never know but it definitely existed before the Domesday survey of 1086 and was almost certainly sited near the present parish church on the hill half a mile (1km) to the west of the later medieval town. Only excavation could provide the tell-tale evidence of the rectangular, sunken floored 'cruck' houses surrounding an open green which might be expected for a small Saxon village. The buildings would probably have consisted of the houses of artisans and tradespeople, the home farm, the thane's (lord's) hall house; the rough hovels of serfs (slaves), a priest's house and a small rectangular church built of wood or 'wattle and daub' and with a thatched roof. There were probably no defences as such. Nearby Lydford, on the other hand, was laid out as a fortified *burgh* (town) by King Alfred the Great in the 880s for defence against the Danes – one of four such towns in Devon (the others being Pilton [Barnstaple], Halwell [near Totnes] and Exeter). It had a regular street pattern, a royal mint and was defended by a huge earth bank to cut off the spur on which it was built.

The new Wessex shire (county) of Devon was divided into around thirty three *hundreds* for administrative purposes sometime in the 10th century. *Ocmund tune* fell under the hundred of *Liwtune* (Lifton) where King Aethelstan held a *Witan* or royal council in 931. Through the hundreds, taxes were collected, armies were raised and law and order enforced – indeed the magistrates court districts are still largely governed by the boundaries established over a thousand years ago. The Saxons were probably largely converted to Christianity by St Augustine's mission from Rome before they conquered Devon and early settlers may have also come into contact with the Celtic missionaries. By the tenth century the church in Devon was well established and governed by the see (bishopric) first of Sherbourne in Dorset and then Crediton from 909. However, in 1050, it was brought under the see of Exeter, along with the whole of Cornwall.

The Danes did eventually come to test Lydford's defences but not until 997, when, according to the Saxon Chronicle, they brought their longboats up the Tamar and 'burning and slaying everything they met' along the route, including Tavistock Abbey which had been founded just twenty years before. But the inhabitants of Lydford stood fast, the great earthen banks served their purpose and the Danes returned to their ships with their plunder. No Danish settlements are known in this part of Devon, even during the time when the Danish king Canute ruled over the entire land, but their legacy of terror will no doubt have lingered on for many generations.

The small settlement of Ocmundtune, meanwhile, probably escaped the ravages of Danish raiders and its inhabitants would have continued their mundane lives until the arrival of the Normans. The village would have been surrounded by the communal cultivation strips of the 'infield' and, beyond them, larger, less frequently cultivated 'outfields' where stock was grazed. Beyond these again would have lain the moorland common lands, to the south, and tracts of heath and woodland, interspersed with scattered farmsteads, to the north – all linked by a network of rough, winding tracks. Here and there would be the remnants of the small Iron Age fields, especially around the moor's edge, and the farms of the Celtic descendants themselves. The wild woods – consisting mainly of oak, ash, beech, elm and holly – was home for the deer and wild boar hunted by the local Saxon nobility and, each autumn, domestic pigs would be released into the woods for *pannage* on the acorns. Managed woodland provided wood for fuel and building, and charcoal for iron working. Large tracts of marshy lowland 'moor' would still have defied the improver's plough and the upland moors would have continued to provide common grazing during the summer months as they had done for some two thousand years before.

AT THE CROSSROADS

Huna stood at the crossroads, recalling the many travellers that he had witnessed passing through the small settlement of Ocmundtune during his long life. He couldn't help wondering where the roads led and imagined the different paths his own life might have taken if he had set off along any of them. The year was 1069, just three years after the famous battle of Hastings when Duke William of Normandy – the Conqueror, had defeated the Saxon Harold I of Wessex. There was unrest in the Southwest with open rebellion against the harsh new Norman order. Huna (*10*) had reached the unusually old age of fifty five. He had lived through a period of great change and upheaval, from the ever-present threat of raids by marauding Danes of his childhood to the recent conquest by their kinsmen – the Normans. He had spent the early part of his life as a serf (slave) to the family of the Saxon thane (lord), the recently deposed Osfers, but was finally given his freedom at a special ceremony one Midsummer's Eve about twenty years before. This had taken place in the presence of priests from the local Minster, led by one called Brown, who conducted the service on that very spot – the cross roads symbolising his freedom to choose his own destiny from thereon.

He remembered all to well the fear instilled in him as a boy by the stories of Danish raids in the area and the first hand accounts of the firestorms, fighting and plunder that had filled him with a mixture of terror and excitement. Then, he would have given anything to join the Saxon warriors he so admired though they would have laughed at the sight of a ten-year-old serf in their midst! Equally ingrained in Huna's memory was his first trip with his master into the great burgh of Lydford – the massive gates that closed the gap between the huge stone-faced banks, the wooden stockade which topped them and the soldiers with shiny metal helmets that patrolled the parapet. The streets were regular and lined with houses. He recalled the ringing of hammer blows on blacksmiths' anvils and the coin dies of the royal mint; the glittering silver pennies they produced and the cries of street traders amid the general hustle and bustle of town life – all so different to his hovel in the small settlement of Ocmundtune.

Rather than soldiering, much of Huna's life had been spent working on the land – a hard, soul-destroying existence for little reward, other than a leaky roof over his head and a meagre diet of coarse bread, cereals, milk and hard cheese on the table. His wife had died many years before while giving birth to their only surviving son, Egbert, who now worked the land on his own account as a churl (free peasant). Huna lived with Egbert and his wife, Alfreda and their five children in a modest house on the edge of the village. He had helped him build it with a sense of pride though, as Egbert had attained far more than he had ever dreamed of for himself – land to till, livestock, a dry roof overhead and, most importantly, freedom. The house consisted of a rectangular hollow in the ground, covered with rough-hewn planks to provide a dry floor and low, timber framed walls, in-filled with wattle and daub panels. A-shaped cruck timbers supported the steeply pitched thatched roof and a hole near the centre allowed the smoke to escape from the open hearth. There were no windows, the only light filtering through the smoke hole and the cracks in the door or from the flickering fire itself. Furnishings were minimal: low wooden platforms for sitting, sleeping and eating; straw-filled mattresses; a loom; cauldron and an array of wooden cooking and eating utensils.

Reconstructed sunken floored house at West Stowe Saxon Village, Suffolk

Sharing the house with a young family meant that the conditions were cramped and noisy. The smoke from the open fire gave Huna frequent coughing attacks, he had lost most of his teeth and his old limbs ached with rheumatism, caused by decades of living and working in damp conditions. He still did what he could though, even if it was only feeding the livestock. There was no way that he could keep up with the oxen pulling the plough as he did when he was a boy, goading them along with a stick while the ploughman guided the iron-shod plough along behind, turning an acre (.4 hectare) strip a day. No longer could he creep into the woods to catch a glimpse of the hunting party, gather sweet honey or climb trees for birds eggs – among the few pleasures in his daily life. His master, on the other hand, had enjoyed a life of hunting, feasting and entertaining in his large hall. As a slave boy, Huna would attend these feasts to serve the guests – noblemen from other villages or churls who gave him service on his land or as soldiers when required. Quantities of ale, mead (made from fermented honey) and even wine from far off lands, accompanied meals of fresh or salt meat, fish, bread, peas, cabbage and fruit. Entertainment from minstrels and storytellers, dice games and riddles around the open hearth would round the evenings off.

Animals weren't the only things hunted in the great wood. There were outlaws, evading the rough justice meted out by the shire or village *moot* courts. If caught, any villager could rightfully kill them so they were understandably elusive! However, the alternative wasn't much better for those facing more severe charges such as murder, theft, arson or treachery. First they had to face trial by ordeal in the nave of the church, perhaps plunging their hand into a cauldron of scalding water to retrieve a stone or holding a red-hot iron bar until it seared their skin. Then the wounds were bandaged. If they had started to heal after three days, they were deemed innocent. If not, they faced a heavy fine, mutilation or even death by hanging. The gallows, erected on the roadside at the edge of the parish, served as a solemn reminder to all passers-by.

Now, as Huna neared the end of his long life, a new foe had appeared on the horizon. The Norman descendants of the Norsemen, who had settled in northern France a century before, had deposed Harold, son of Earl Godwin of Wessex. With their small but well-armed and organised army, they were now consolidating their power in the Southwest following an uprising centred on Exeter. One of their most powerful barons, Baldwin – son of Count Gilbert of Brionne in Normandy and husband of the Conqueror's cousin Emma – had been appointed Sheriff of Devon. He had already been tasked with overseeing the building of a royal castle at Exeter and was keen to establish his personal presence in the county. Baldwin had chosen a spot near Saxon Ocmundtune as the capital of his new barony. Not only was it geographically central to the two hundred-odd rural manors he had been granted by William as a reward for his support, but it sat on one of the main routes west into Cornwall and on the confluence of other important routes. Dartmoor, to the south, was still largely impenetrable to all but the moormen who knew it intimately. The site chosen was by coincidence (or perhaps by design?) that of the old Celtic shrine of the sacred grove. The natural spur and spring-fed stream beside it still held some deep-seated meaning in the native folklore and loomed over the Okement valley upstream of Ocmundtune. For these strangers to come and build a great castle on its summit was somehow symbolic and would send a powerful message to any potential dissenters (*11*).

Huna witnessed the dramatic arrival of mounted Norman knights and infantry with a mixture of fear and awe. The cavalrymen especially looked formidable on their huge warhorses in their knee-length chain mail shirts and with their conical iron helmets, broad swords and the bosses of their long shields glinting in the sunlight. They spoke with a foreign tongue but shouted orders contemptuously in broken English. By sundown they had pressed some fifty men and boys from the district into a labour gang to start on the construction works. They were well prepared and had brought their own craftsmen and many of the tools required for the work. At sunrise the following day they set to work. The earthworks progressed rapidly. First a deep ditch was cut across the tip of the spur and around the sides and front and the excavated shaley material was heaped on top to form a steep-sided motte (mound). Meanwhile, a wooden stockade was constructed on the lower side of the ditch to form a bailey (enclosed courtyard) with a fighting platform around the inside and strong wooden gates (*12*). A range of timber buildings including barracks; stables and a hall were built within the bailey while work started on a substantial stone tower on the motte. The whole job was completed within weeks and the walls finished outside with coats of lime-washed plaster, not only to keep out driving rain but also to stand out clearly in the landscape as an unquestionable statement – the Normans were here to stay!

A NEW TOWN IS BORN

By the time of the Domesday Survey of 1086, most of Devon's Saxon thanes, including Osfers, had been deposed. The new Norman order had been imposed across the South West, in spite of unrest and various rebellions – at least four led by three illegitimate sons of the late King Harold. William himself experienced Saxon contempt for the new order first hand when he arrived at the gates of besieged Exeter in 1068 and an inhabitant 'having bared himself, standing on the walls, disturbed the ears with a sound from his lower parts'! Whether he or his followers experienced such spirited resistance from the inhabitants of Ocmundtune is not known.

One thing is sure; life for most people who worked the land went on much as before. Members of the new Norman nobility were comparatively few and lived apart from their feudal tenants. This Norman/Saxon class division is well illustrated in our words for livestock: cow, sheep, pig, deer etc – all of Saxon origin while their meat derivatives are beef, mutton, pork and venison – all from French roots, demonstrating the distinction between producer and consumer in Norman society. Nevertheless, they depended on each other, the one to produce food, provide labour on the Lord's land and military service when required, the other to provide land and security.

Baldwin no doubt had more than a military stronghold in mind when he established Okehampton Castle. By 1086, Domesday records the existence of a market – one of only two recorded in Devon – and four burgesses (townsmen). It also mentions a mill – also something of a rarity in Devon at that time – so, clearly, he was keen to encourage commerce and the development of a town with free traders who would provide taxes in return for certain privileges. The villains (tenant farmers) living on the scattered farms throughout the parish, on the other hand, still had to fulfil their feudal obligation of working on his home farm for so many days each year. Baldwin also had sub-tenants for the manors of Kigbeare and Chichacott. He granted Kigbeare to his steward, Rainer, and Chichacott to Roger de Molis, whose family originated from Meules, one of Baldwin's estates in Normandy. Baldwin himself had to pay taxes and provide military support to the King in return for his own grants of land which, like most baronies, were scattered across the County as a safeguard against insurrection from a consolidated power base. In this way William gained a firm grasp of his newly conquered realm in a fairly short space of time and with relatively few direct supporters.

His next task was to quantify his acquisitions and assess them for taxation purposes and so the Domesday Survey was launched. It provides the most comprehensive list of property and people we have for this period although it inevitably omits non-taxable land (the wastes of Dartmoor for instance) and non-land-holding religious establishments. Using data from the survey, it has been estimated that the total population of Devon in 1086 stood at somewhere around the 80,000 mark. Using the same formula, the population of Okehampton and its immediate surroundings probably stood at around 320. By comparison, Lydford town had a population of around 400, including 69 burgesses, even allowing for 'fifty houses laid bare since the Conquest', and Exeter around 1,500.

The entry for Okehampton in the Exon Domesday reads as follows:

"Baldwin the Sheriff has a manor called Ochenemitona which Osfers held in the reign of Edward and it rendered geld for 3 virgates and 1 ferding. This 30 ploughs can till. Thereof Baldwin has 1 virgate and 1 ferding and 4 ploughs in demesne and the villains 2 virgates and 20 ploughs. There Baldwin has 31 villains, 11 borders, 18 serfs, 6 swine herds, 1 rouncy, 52 beasts, 80 sheep, 1 mill which renders 6s.8d. a year, wood 3 leagues in length by 1 league in breadth, 5 acres of meadow, pasturage 1 league in length by half a league in breadth and on his land stands the castle of Ochenemitone. There Baldwin has 4 burgesses and a market which render 4s. a year. This manor is worth with its appurtenances £10 and when Baldwin received it was worth £8."

That of Kigbeare reads:

Baldwin has a manor called Cacheberga which Sewin (or Sawin) held TRE., and it paid geld for 1 virgate. This 5 ploughs can till. Raner (Rainer) holds it of Baldwin and has in demesne 1 ferding and 1 plough and the villeins have 3 ferdings and 3 ploughs. There Raner has 6 villeins, 5 bordars, 1 serf, 5 beasts, 30 sheep, 3 swine, 2 acres of wood(land)*, 12 acres of meadow and 20 acres of pasture. Worth 30s. a year and was worth 20s. when he received it.*

And for Chichacott:

Baldwin has a manor called Cicecota which Brismar held TRE., and it paid geld for ? virgate. This 3 ploughs can till. Now Roger holds it of Baldwin. There Roger has 1 plough in demesne, and the villeins till with 2 oxen. There Roger has 4 villeins, 1 bordar, 1 serf, 13 beasts, 3 swine, 32 sheep, 30 acres of wood(land)*, 3 acres of meadow, and 3 acres of pasture. Worth 15s. a year, and was worth the same when Baldwin received it.*

A virgate was a land measurement of anything between 15 and 80 acres (6-32 hectares)

A ferding was a quarter of a virgate. A league was about 9 miles (15km). Demesne land was the lord's home farm. *Villains* were tenant farmers on the lord's land, while *borders* were simple cottagers. *Serfs* were slaves and accounted for in a similar manner to livestock. A *rouncy* was a small horse.

Precisely where the market and early town referred to in the entry for Okehampton were sited, nobody knows. It could have been at the castle gates, thereby enjoying its protection and patronage to the disadvantage of the Saxon settlement of Ocmundtune (*13*) or it may have become established between the two rivers in its present location – midway between castle and church and straddling the main highway. What is now High Street leading off the western end of Fore (Saxon *vor* – 'through') Street is another contender, leading as it does away from the vicinity of the Church site towards the medieval town and showing evidence of early 'burgage plots' stretching back behind the houses fronting it. Before New Road was built during the turnpike trust era (around 1820), this was the main highway from the town towards Launceston. It was formerly known as Sharp ('steep') or Shob (Saxon 'sheep') Hill. Two sunken lanes – Darkey Lane and Stoney Park Lane – running parallel to it – are evidently of some antiquity. Together with Broadmoor and Maggies (now Ranelagh Road) lanes to the north and east of the church and one passing close by its west gate, they appear to form a grid pattern. Could this represent the remnants of a network of 'streets' from the early scattered Saxon settlement?

Over the next two centuries there was a steady growth in farming and trade in the area. An improved climate, the stability of the new order and favourable economic conditions encouraged more waste land to be cultivated, even the slopes of Dartmoor above the 1,000 foot contour level. The infant town of Okehampton grew under the patronage of the Sheriff and his heirs. When Baldwin died in 1090 he left four sons. Guiger was a monk at Bec Abbey in Normandy while William, Robert and Richard were all actively involved with his estates and were also sheriffs. Robert concentrating on affairs back in Normandy, while William and Richard went on to assist with the conquest of south Wales. Okehampton Castle was never the permanent residence of any of them but Richard is said to have been the founder of the 'ancient customs' referred to in a charter granted to the borough by Robert Courtenay after he came into the estate in 1219.

The establishment of a Cistercian priory at nearby Brightley in 1133 also demonstrated Richard's interest in the young town. On the 3rd May 1136, a prior, also named Richard, and twelve monks came from Waverley Abbey in Surrey. The priory was short-lived, however, as the damp conditions, together with the deaths of their founder the following year and of their first prior, is said to have discouraged them so much that they left in 1141. Hardship and isolation were central to the Cistercian order and they were also excellent agriculturists. This combination of circumstances must, therefore, have been deemed sufficiently catastrophic to justify abandoning Okehampton in favour of the greener pastures of the borders of Devon and Dorset where they went on to found Forde Abbey on land given by Richard fitz Baldwin's sister Adeliza. The priory chapel of St. Mary continued in use until the Reformation however, and was attached to Sampford Courtenay Church even though it was in Okehampton parish. Remnants of this chapel still survive among farm buildings near Brightley Bridge but are on private land.

It is likely that the earliest church would have been built of timber. If Okehampton followed the same pattern as other parishes in the district, this would probably have been re-built in stone at some point in the twelfth or thirteenth century although there is no surviving fabric or record of an earlier building. However, the fact that the church stands half a mile away from the new town at the bottom of the hill strongly suggests that it occupied an earlier consecrated site. Although Bishop Bronescombe is recorded as consecrating the church in 1261, the practice of re-consecrating established churches was not uncommon at the time. In fact, Bronscombe is known to have consecrated around fifty churches in three years. The first recorded vicar was Robert de Denvorn in 1233 and in 1239 the living was granted to the Benedictine priory of Cowick, Exeter along with the castle chapel. The remote position of the church became a problem for the townsfolk though and at some point the chantry chapel of St. James was built in the centre. It is probably the 'free chapel' for which Reginald Courtenay was granted a licence in 1178. Baldwin, a monk of Forde Abbey, was appointed as chaplain. It was independent of the parish church and the portreeve and others acted as wardens and appointed the chaplain who's main role was to say masses for souls of the dead.

None of Baldwin's sons had any male heirs and so their sister, Adeliza, succeeded them. The castle and other estates then passed through the families of various heiresses until 1173 when the surviving heiress, Hawisia, married Reginald Courtenay – so beginning the long association between that family and the castle. Robert Courtenay's charter confirmed the old rights of the burgesses and granted various other privileges including the right to elect a *provost* (portreeve) and an assistant known as the *cryer*. The provost would collect market tolls for the lord as well as representing the interests of the burgesses. Soon after they were also granted a fair to be held each year on the vigil and feast of St. James the Apostle (24th - 25th July). The translation of Robert's charter runs as follows:–

Know ye that I Robert de Courtenay have given and granted and by this present deed confirmed, with the assent and consent of Mary my wife and of my heirs, to my Burgesses of my free borough of Okehampton all their tenements and free customs which they had in the time of Richard the son of Baldwin and of Robert the King's son Matilda of Averenges his wife and of Hawisia of Courtenay my mother, in the Borough and in lands outside the Borough. Yielding therefor yearly for every burgage to me and to my heirs, by the hands of my Portreeve of the Borough, at the Festival of St Michael 12d. for all services and demands pertaining to me and to my heirs and to them and to their heirs. To have and to hold of me and my heirs by right of inheritance freely, quietly, peaceably and honorably for evermore in wood and in plain, in ways and paths, in marshes and in common pastures, in waters and in mills, and in all places where I and my heirs may reasonably warrant. We have also granted that the Burgesses shall yearly, of their own council, elect and depose a Provost and a Cryer; the Provost shall be quit of his rent, the Cryer of sixpence. If a plea relating to the lord arises in the Borough, it ought to be ended within the same. If anyone of the Borough shall forfeit an amercement to the lord he should be quit for 12d.; if a habitual offender, he shall be chastised by the judgment and advice of the Burgesses and of my Seneschal (steward) *according to the gravity of the offence. If anyone take a new burgage, he shall have house-bote in my wood of Okehampton by the advice of my Seneschal and my good men. If the Burgesses or their children wish to marry or be given in marriage, they may quietly do so wherever they will. Every Burgess may have his sow and four little pigs quit of pannage in my wood of Okehampton. None, unless he be of the Borough, shall buy green hide in the Borough nor do any retail trade. The Provost shall collect the toll and shall have 12d. from the toll and the quittance of his rent (gablum) for this service. The toll shall be: for a horse 1d., for an ox 1/2d., for five sheep 1d., for five pigs 1d., for corn and grain nothing. If anyone shall buy or sell within the longstone or [yleneyete], he must pay toll. If anyone evades the toll, he shall be quit on paying: for a farthing 5s., for a halfpenny 10s., and for a penny 20s. If a Burgess wishes to depart he may sell his burgage, if he will, to whom he wishes, except to religious houses. He shall depart without challenge on giving to the lord 12d., to the Provost 4d., and to the Borough 4d.; but if a Burgess die, his widow and heirs may quietly receive his tenements. If anyone desires the liberty of the Borough and is such as can be received, in the first year he shall pay to the lord 4d. and to the Borough 4d.; in the second year he shall pay 4d. to the lord only and, in the third year, he shall take his burgage or pay gablum and go away. If anyone carries away the debt of any Burgess, the Burgesses may take the chattels of the debter in their town and retain them until he has lawfully satisfied them. My Burgesses shall be quit of toll through all Devon, where I and my heirs can and should lawfully warrant them. None, unless of free condition, shall stand in law against my Burgesses. All rents, amerciaments and issues of the Borough shall be paid to me or my heirs by the hand of the Provost. For this my gift, grant and confirmation the aforesaid Burgesses have given me 10 marks as consideration.*

With these special privileges and freedoms being granted to the Burgesses at the height of the oppressive feudal system, it is not difficult to see why town life proved so attractive. As a consequence, the town and market grew to such an extent that they soon threatened the pre-eminence of Lydford and the burgesses there had cause to complain of unfair competition. The growth of the neighbouring towns of Tavistock, with its great Benedictine abbey, and Launceston could hardly have helped Lydford's fortunes either.

A COMMON BOND

The year was 1303 and King Edward I was on the throne. The castle had been largely re-built by the Courtenays who were gaining power, wealth and prestige across the country. The town was growing in size and prosperity in its new location on the level ground between the two rivers and was governed by the Portreeve and burgesses. Meanwhile, peasant farmers were enjoying relative productivity and prosperity in the district, thanks to a spell of settled weather and increasing demand from rapid population growth, although, unlike their neighbours in the borough, they were still tied rigidly to the Courtenays by the feudal system.

In the peasant settlement of Byrham (*14*) against the moor above the castle, Hawisia fetched more wood for the open hearth in her small, single storied

Impression of a medieval longhouse against the moor. Note the central opening to the cross passage and the drain hole from the shippon in the lower gable wall. The small cow is of the type that would have been housed within

home. At over one thousand feet above sea level, Byrham was one of the first permanent settlements at this altitude since the Bronze Age some two thousand years before. But, in spite of the more favourable climate, it was still be a bleak place to live on a wild winter's night when a northwest wind blew at the door!.

Hawisia *(15)* was twenty-six years old. Her husband, John, had died three years before at the age of thirty-one, leaving her to raise three girls on her own – well, almost. John's mother, Joanne, lived with her but she was more hindrance than help and always thought she knew best – "John would'n 'av done it like that"! John was just as bad. He had always seemed to criticise how she reared the children – "You ought to listen to mother" he would say, "her knows a thing or two about chilern" That was true, she had brought twelve into the world, enough to have started another borough, if they had all survived! Hawisia's eldest daughter Mary, aged twelve, was in service with the Courtenays down at the castle although John had always wanted her to take Holy Orders. At least, there, she had security and a sound roof over her head. Hawisia could really have done with her help around the home but things were just too tight to feed another mouth. Her younger sister, Joanna, once the apple of her father's eye, was barely old enough at seven to be of much help either but she did her best and looked after her baby sister Hannah with a care beyond her age. This trait gave Hawisia hope that she might receive such love and attention when old age slowed her down. She prayed that she would find her a good husband with whom she could bear children of her own one-day. In spite of Joanna's mothering instincts, she still worried about the safety of little Hannah around the fire and the animals while she worked outside.

Such concerns were at the back of Hawisia's mind, however. Her whole future was uncertain as she faced eviction from her land and home to make way for the Courtenay's new Deer Park *(16)*. Despite her worst fears of destitution, she was not bitter. Peasants did not question the social order or their lack of liberty. It had always been thus and she enjoyed the security that the feudal system provided – until now that was. A dozen or so of her neighbours from the scattered farmsteads along the hill slope faced a similar fate – brothers, cousins and in-laws – all had to find new lands. With them would go another part of her security, the mutual support network that went with living within such a community. Each farmstead was linked to the others by a system of drove ways and they helped each other with building, labouring and stock herding. They also shared precious commodities such as ploughs and the oxen that pulled them, a sledge for moving boulders and wood and turf for the fires and the packhorse, which took, produce down to the market.

As the families had grown over the previous century, the buildings had been improved or extended to accommodate them. First simple rectangular wooden houses with timber crucks supporting thatched roofs were constructed. These were eventually replaced by buildings with more substantial, dry-stone walls of about two metres in height that enclosed and supported crucks set into the ground (*17*). Other houses and byres were added to each farm as the families grew. Hawisia lived in one of the more substantial dwellings, as John was an eldest son. It had two living rooms – a hall and an inner chamber beyond – on the higher side of a cross-passage and a cattle house or *shippon* on the lower side. The floors in the living area consisted of compacted subsoil, covered with rushes. The small rooms were open to the roof and very dark. The pith of rushes dipped in goose fat or tallow provided some light after dark and narrow window slits let a little light in during the day but, without glass to keep out some of the wind, they had to be blocked or shuttered for much of the time. Neither these nor the ill-fitting door did much to reduce the draughts though.

The open hearth burned on a granite slab, partly surrounded by a horseshoe-shaped wattle screen in the centre of the floor, towards the inner end of the main living area. This provided some light and warmth but the benefits were rather outweighed by the choking smoke that filled the higher levels of the room before escaping through the thatch. Most of the cooking was done over this fire using a primitive spit and iron crocks, which had to be scoured out with gravel collected from the river. The family diet was inevitably restricted to what could be produced on the land as there was no money as such to purchase anything from the market (*18*) and taking of game from the lord's demesne was a highly risky business with a maximum penalty of death.

At least the produce was fresh when in season – vegetables such as leeks, onions and cabbages from a plot by the house provided ingredients for 'pot-herbs' or *pottage*. Bread was baked in a small clay oven, heated with lighted faggots which were then raked out to make way for the doe. This was formed from the flour of rye or wheat, ground in a hand *quern* (mill). There was a water mill by the castle, belonging to the Courtenays, where corn could be taken for grinding but the miller and lord took a goodly proportion of the resultant flour for their trouble. Like most people in the district and town, Hawisia kept a pig which was fattened-up during the summer and killed and salted in the autumn to provide a supply of meat throughout the winter. Any unpleasant tastes were masked by the addition of herbs, vegetables and leftover bread. The odd rabbit (one of the more popular introductions of the Normans!) also found its way onto the table to provide extra variety. Salmon and trout from the Okement provided flesh on the days when the Church dictated that no meat should be eaten, for instance during fasts leading up to religious feasts and every Friday. In addition there were dairy products from the cows, sheep and goats milk, whey (buttermilk) and curds (solids) which were eaten directly or made into hard cheese. Pleasures were few and strong barley ale provided a little welcome elevation on occasions when friends and family came round to exchange gossip and tell stories by the fireside of ghostly apparitions or the devil and his whisht hounds up on the moors.

Also within the living room, which measured around 16 feet by 13 feet (5m x 4m), were items of primitive wooden furniture mounted on small stakes driven into the floor. There was a raised table, some benches and a bed for the children. A vertical loom stood by the door to allow enough light for Hawisia to weave the coarse cloth with which the family's clothes and blankets were made when work on the farm allowed. First the wool had to be spun using a hand spindle. This was a task that could be carried out while sitting by the fire after a hard day's labour. The resultant yarn was then dyed, using various plants and substances, before being woven. Hawisia wore a long woollen gown of russet brown; a sleeveless tunic and a hooded cape called a capuchon. When the weather was particularly cold she would throw on a sheep skin cloak and wear a woollen hat. The coarse fabric gown was rather uncomfortable so she wore linen undergarments to reduce the chaffing. Her feet were clad in stockings and leather boots, covered with wooden patens to protect them from sharp stones and the spade edge as well as helping to keep them dry.

Beyond a stone dividing wall lay a smaller 'inner' room where food and produce was stored and where Hawisia and her mother-in-law slept on raised wooden beds covered with animal skins – rather smelly but cosy. One of the few benefits of the all-pervading smoke from the hearth was that it killed off bacteria and masked smells. Just as well as personal hygiene was unheard of! The 'cross-passage' between the two opposing external doors at the opposite end of the living area was partly screened-off by a wattle partition. The passage provided shared access to both the hall and the shippon (cow house) beyond. The shippon measured 22 feet by 13 feet (7 m x 4 m) and consisted of another single storey area, open to the roof. A central open drain lead to a small opening through the lower end gable so that the cow dung and urine could be washed out. There were feeding mangers mounted on stakes along the outer walls on either side and rows of posts to which the cattle could be tethered when brought in. Their breath provided a bit of extra warmth during the winter months – to some extent making up for the extra smells they brought.

Outside there was a yard where stock could be corralled and sorted, various wooden pens, a pigsty, wood rick, turf store and dung heap. Human waste was added to that of the animals and all put back on the land – nothing was wasted.

The fields were ploughed in *lynchets* – artificially created cultivation terraces – using a metal-tipped wooden plough pulled by a team of oxen with one man leading them and another steadying the plough behind. Crops of barley, rye and wheat were grown and, once cultivated, the land was allowed to lie fallow (uncultivated) for a period of time to ensure continued productivity. Stock was grazed on the rest although the keep was supplemented during the summer months by access to common grazing on the adjoining moors. The tenants of Byrham also had *pannage* (the right to feed pigs on acorns) in the lord's woods during the autumn. Though the ploughing and other field work was generally done by men, Hawisia's daily routine was equally hard – rearing and tending stock, milking, hand grinding corn, keeping poultry, cleaning, cooking, spinning and weaving.

In addition to paying a proportion of her produce to the lord as rent and another tenth to the church for a *tithe*, she had to give so many days service to the lord, such as stock droving or working on his land. This obligation made it difficult to provide food for her own table at times but the worst consequence of the feudal system had been the loss of John's best cow as *herriot* (payment of the 'best beast' to the lord) on his death.

Hawisia stared into the flames of the fire and her thoughts turned again to the future. She wondered whether she'd still have a roof over her head when winter set in. But tomorrow was the Feast of St. James and there was to be a great fair down in the town. Perhaps she would find a suitable husband for Mary there. This would also provide her with a son-in-law, a new home and the security she desperately sought.

Meanwhile, down at the castle, Mary was busy with preparations for a banquet in the great hall to mark the Eve of St. James. Watching over the frantic activity was Lady Eleanor Courtenay (*19*). She too was a widow. Her husband, Lord Hugh Courtenay, had died twelve years before and the castle had been in Royal hands until her son, Hugh, came of age in 1297. He was a ward of King Edward during his minority but was now firmly in control of the family's vast estates. The Courtenays had been fortunate in inheriting the castle and other estates as a result of an earlier marriage into Sheriff Baldwin's family and had recently added to them through a similar relationship with the de Redvers family – the Earls of Devon – whose principle residence had been Tiverton Castle. Both family lines had come to an end for want of a male heir and so the Courtenays had inherited through the female line. Fortunately, Hugh and Agnes already had two sons but Eleanor was naturally anxious that they should survive long enough to bear sons of their own to ensure that the Courtenay line would grow and prosper at the expense of rival families in the region. For a suitable dowry, any daughters might also find security and provide further investments for the future!

The Earldom should have come with the de Redvers estates but, unfortunately, the King had allowed this to lapse. Hugh was determined to win it back but first he had to prove himself worthy. Tiverton had become the family's principal residence but Okehampton, with its picturesque setting and good hunting, was held in great affection by the family. Eleanor had many happy memories of riding out through the old castle gates with her late husband to enjoy the chase. The castle had altered considerably since then however and

Reconstruction of Okehampton Castle following the re-building of around 1300. (English Heritage)

he would hardly have recognised it now. Young Hugh had had most of it re-built with all the latest conveniences – numerous en-suite *garderobes* (latrines) and built-in fireplaces – both unheard of in the neighbourhood hitherto. He was anxious to impress.

The exterior of the castle was especially impressive to anyone approaching up the valley from the town. Its towering walls, plastered and lime washed, gleamed white against the trees and sky and colourful pennants streamed and fluttered from the tops of the gatehouses and turrets. Whether the visitor was a tenant coming to pay rent, a burgess making a plea at court or a noble coming to stay in the fine apartments as a guest, they could not fail to be impressed by such grandeur. First they would enter through the outer, *barbican*, gate and into the walled passage beyond. This also served as a defensive feature – a deadly 'killing ground' for any assailants who managed to get past the barbican gate and then tried to attack the main gatehouse at the top of the slope. The gatehouse was a fine structure with a drawbridge spanning a defensive ditch, a portcullis and high vaulted roof. Beyond this again lay the bailey courtyard. A door to the right gave access to the guardroom and an antechamber to the great hall where visitors would wait to be summoned in. Above were the steward's office and a room over the gatehouse where the machinery for raising the portcullis and drawbridge was housed.

The great hall was approached via a flight of steps to the 'high end' where a raised platform or *dais* provided a suitably elevated position for Hugh when holding court or for all the family when a banquet was in progress. Along one side of the hall was a stone bench for others to sit. Trestles were set up in the centre when required for banqueting and a huge open hearth was kept roaring just in front of the dais. The smoke escaped through a *louver* in the splendid timber and slate roof. Such open fires had been the centre of life in great halls since time immemorial and shared by lords and servants alike. With the advent of enclosed fireplaces and chimneys in rich households however, physical class divisions were becoming more apparent. Hugh and his wife, Agnes, had a private apartment or *solar* above the buttery at the far end of the hall, where they could withdraw for privacy after a feast (*20*). The walls of the hall were plastered and painted with coats of arms and hung with large tapestries and hunting trophies. Large glazed windows, with wide splays, let ample light into the hall during the day while numerous candles and the fire illuminated it at night. Rush matting covered the floor and sweet-smelling herbs helped mask the less pleasant smells. Any leftovers from banquets, which were not scavenged from the floor by the dogs or eaten by the servants, were later distributed to any poor waiting at the castle gate.

At the far end, a wooden screen hid the working areas beyond. The buttery (from the French *bouteille* – bottle), beneath the solar, was where the steward directed the male servants and oversaw the provisions and preparation of food and drink for the guests. A passageway led from the screens passage to the kitchens. It was covered so that the food didn't get cold en-route. There was a gap between the hall and the kitchens as a precaution against fire spreading and to give access to the wall walk along the top of the defensive *curtain* (surrounding) wall. The first kitchen had an open hearth, an ash pit to keep food warm and two cooking fires, one for spit roasting meat and poultry and the other for stews and broths. The second kitchen had two great ovens for baking bread and pies. These were fuelled with burning faggots which were raked out when the temperature was sufficient. There was also a large larder where food was kept cool.

On the *motte* (mound) above, the sturdy stone *keep* (strong tower) of Baldwin's castle had been extended and now consisted of two parts providing storage on the ground floor and some fine apartments above with splendid views over the old deer park. If the castle were ever attacked however, the keep's thick walls would have to provide the last line defence though it was doubtful whether the defenders would have been able to hold-out for too long without a separate water supply, kitchens or a chapel to nourish the spirit. A spiral staircase, built into the thickness of the wall in one corner gave access to the upper floor and roof parapet. Down the other side of the bailey were the chapel and priest's lodging and a range of guests' lodgings over servants' quarters. The chapel wasn't large but was brightly decorated with painted walls and woodwork. Two stained glass windows on the bailey side and one in the outer wall cast their coloured hues across the patterned and glazed tile floor and an alter rail divided the chancel from the main body of the chapel. The castle chaplain conducted holy mass each morning, attended by the family and other members of the household. Eleanor spent many hours in the chapel in solemn contemplation or listening to the priests singing chants. It provided a welcome haven away from the hustle and bustle of the castle and she felt closer to her dear husband there. Although wealth could not buy immortality, it could help to ensure a place in Heaven and so a priest was paid to say mass for Hugh's soul down in the town's chapel of St. James. The family would also attend mass at the parish church on religious festivals when they were in residence.

The lodgings beyond were lavishly appointed with built-in fireplaces and large windows overlooking the river and parkland beyond. The plastered walls were painted and hung with rich tapestries. The beds had curtains suspended from poles extending from the walls to reduce draughts and to provide some privacy from the personal servants who slept in the same room as their masters and mistresses – male servants for men, female for women. The latrine arrangements were particularly sophisticated here, one garderobe even boasted a built-in hand basin adjacent. Things were not quite so good for the servants who had to avail themselves of the facilities from their quarters below as they shared the same chutes. They also had the unpleasant task of emptying the cesspits, but, compared to sanitary arrangements in most households in the district, even their conditions must have seemed luxurious.

Inevitably these lodgings remained empty for much of the year as the itinerant household followed the family around. A small retinue of staff remained to look after the castle and local affairs – the steward, constable, bailiff, some servants and a small permanent garrison of men-at-arms in case of trouble. When the family were in residence however, the travelling household of family, servants and officials swelled the numbers considerably. On the occasions that Hugh held court, the castle was filled to capacity by around sixty household and administrative servants, eight knights, forty esquires (trainee knights), a dozen or so lawyers, eight priests and two or three damsels (*21*). Apart from Eleanor and Agnes, a few personal servants and the ever-popular damsels, the household was predominantly male. Agnes supervised the household affairs on Hugh's behalf, ably assisted by Eleanor who still commanded considerable respect from the time when she had been the principal lady of the household. The damsels were the daughters of other noble families and Eleanor and Agnes ensured that they received a thorough grounding in the skills of household management as well as the arts and chivalry. The code of chivalry prevented any openly 'improper' conduct towards these young ladies but what went on behind closed doors was another matter of course! It was not just the damsels who attracted the attention of all those men. Servants had little choice than to put up with abuse and young Mary had had her share of unwanted attention.

However, young Hugh took his position and responsibilities very seriously, if a little too earnestly sometimes. He would not enter into the dice games or singing and dancing around the hearth that the knights and squires enjoyed so much, preferring his own company and holy books. The family chaplain, Ralph, with whom he had formed a close Christian bond, had taught him Latin as a boy. Such studies were usually only available to young men unless a girl was to take up holy orders or was of noble birth and, even then, reading was restricted to religious texts, lest any woman should get ideas 'above her station'. Girls in the castle generally spent their time learning needlework skills, weaving, singing, playing music or dancing. Hugh and Agnes had two sons, John aged three and baby Hugh. Hugh prayed that one of them would one day inherit everything he had built-up and succeed to the Earldom of Devon – the title that should rightfully have been his then – and that the other would be given a senior role in the Church. To hold power in both the affairs of church and state was the Courtenays' ongoing mission.

Not that the family's relationship with the Church had always been that good. Eleanor's late husband, for instance, had once fallen out with the monks of Forde Abbey – the house founded by his ancestors and had raided their cattle and driven them out onto Dartmoor near Okehampton. He had been rather hot-headed and impetuous at times, but then, he was the most powerful man in the County so, apart from the King and God who was there to fear? He wasn't so deluded, however, as to ignore the important business of making money to build-up and protect the family's possessions. If that meant granting charters and striking deals with the local burgesses or other landowners, presiding over manorial courts here, there and everywhere and, if necessary, going to war, that was all part of his feudal role. If he had neglected such duties, his rivals would soon have challenged the Courtenay superiority.

Then there was the equally important business of entertaining guests and enjoying noble pursuits such as swordsmanship, jousting, and falconry and, above all else, hunting. Old Hugh had prepared the way for a great new deer park by exchanging the grazing rights of the town's folk in his woods to the south of the castle with rights over the wastes which lay between the cultivated settlements of Byrham and the Royal Forest of Dartmoor. Young Hugh was now extending the hunting chase by evicting the tenants of Byrham to create a park of some 1,700 acres (700 hectares) – the envy of the whole county. *(22)* One of Eleanor's own special touches to the refurbished castle commemorated her late husband in a very personal but practical way. She had had two bells cast. The largest was inscribed around the top in old English script with the words "WE WERE BOTH MADE TO WAKE ELEANOR FOR TO CATCH GAME" and the other with "BUT DO BY MY ADVICE THINK ON HUGH'S SOUL AND SO WAS HIS NAME" *(23)*. A day's hunting started before dawn when the grooms and kennel boys prepared the horses and hounds for the day ahead and the park keepers checked the park for poachers and any new hazards as well as the whereabouts of deer herds and game. The hunting party would assemble by the main gate at first light and ride out into the park, led by Lord Hugh – woe betide anyone who dared to ride ahead of him! Although Eleanor still enjoyed the sport she tired quickly and tended to leave such exertions to the younger members of the household.

Today though, the entertainment was to be in the meadows by the castle where the stage was set for jousting and an archery contest and would culminate in the great hall where there was to be a lavish banquet accompanied by music and storytelling. There was an excited air about the castle as frantic preparations were being made. Squires busily prepared their masters' armour, equipment and weapons while servants and kitchen hands rushed around in readiness for the feast under the watchful eye of Eleanor and the steward and cooks. Sides of beef, a wild boar, poultry, fish, cheeses, vegetables, sauces, bread and sweetmeats – to be washed down by large quantities of mead, ale and wine – all had to be prepared in the great kitchens and the buttery. Then there was the entertainment to organise – minstrels and dancers rehearsed in the great hall while the jester tried out some new riddles and japes on the steward who really wanted to get on with his work. It was his duty to see that all ran smoothly and to keep a close eye on the servants and children of the guests lest the temptation of all that food should be too great! After all, the household had been fasting for the last week in the run-up to the great feast.

Hawisia's daughter, Mary, was looking forward to the following day as much as anyone as she would be allowed to join her mother and sisters down in the town for St. James's fair and have a rare opportunity to enjoy some entertainment first hand. St. James's Fair was the main event in the town's calendar and, along with the market that accompanied it, would draw people from far and wide. When the day finally arrived, like the scene at the castle the day before, the town was bustling with activity from first light as the burgesses set-up their stalls and prepared their wares. Drovers brought cows, horses, sheep and pigs from the neighbouring farms and villages along the twisting, dusty lanes and into the main street where they were penned in by wattle hurdles. There were chickens, ducks and geese running loose, penned or being carried, squawking noisily, by their legs. Children and dogs ran around excitedly and the noise and stench were almost overpowering!

Elizabeth Brock (*24*) witnessed the mayhem from the door of her bakery. Her husband, Richard the baker, had been laid to rest for two years now but she carried on the trade with the help of her nephew, John. Sadly, she had never had a child of her own to take on the business and, at the age of forty-five, it was too late to find a husband and try again. In any case, John was as good as her own since she had brought him up after her sister and her husband had died of dysentery, contracted through drinking foul water from the well in their back yard, some fifteen years ago. He had finished his apprenticeship with Richard just before his death and now took on much of the hard work, including the early mornings that Elizabeth so hated.

Elizabeth was a well-liked and respected member of the community and had a jolly character to match her portly stature and ruddy complexion but her worst trait was gossiping. If anyone wanted to hear the latest news or scandal they only had to call for a loaf or some cakes and she would willingly go into every detail with relish while poor John slaved away at the ovens. As well as baking bread, pies and cakes for sale on the stall at the front, people often brought their own meals in to be baked. This was the perfect excuse for a chinwag, accompanied by a few home-brewed ales of course! Baking and brewing weren't Elizabeth's only talents. She was also the local midwife and healer. As well as delivering almost half the town's population into the world, she had seen a few leave it in her time, in spite of her best efforts to restore them to health. She was the original 'old wife', revered and sometimes feared lest she should cast the 'evil eye' on anyone who upset her. In the absence of any trained medical practitioner in the town, however, her charms, potions and incantations were much in demand as disease and illness were all too common without proper sanitation. Many of her medicinal plants were gathered from the hedgerows and woods around the town and she also grew a variety of herbs in a plot that stretched down to the West Okement river at the back of her house.

Like those of her neighbours along the single main street, Elizabeth's narrow back garden or *burgage plot* covered about an acre (0.4 hectare) and provided vegetables for the pot as well as space for chickens to run and to rear a litter of pigs each year. There were dung heaps and wood ricks where faggots and furze were stored for the fuel-hungry ovens. The house itself was one of the more substantial in the town, although it was only single storied and timber framed it was built on a solid stone foundation. The framework was filled with wattle and daub panels and supported a thatched roof with a smoke hole in the ridge. There was a good-sized gap around the bake-house at the back, with its constantly lit fires, as an added precaution against the ever-present risk of fire amid the close-packed timber and thatched houses. The shop frontage had a rectangular opening adjacent to the front door, covered by a shutter which was dropped down on market days to form a stall on which to display the bakery's produce to passers by. Although Elizabeth was relatively prosperous, glazing was beyond her means so all of the narrow windows had shutters to keep draughts out. Light was supplied by candles and rush dips and, of course, there was the central domestic open hearth in the main hall. The house ran parallel with the street and had the same basic plan as the 'long houses' of Byrham. From the street door, the shop was to the left of the cross passage and the hall, parlour and an inner chamber were off to the right of the oak screen which ran across to the back door. The chamber had a small loft over where John slept and, besides the bake-house, there was a lean-to scullery and brew-house to the rear.

To the front was the wide main street and market place, its centre marked by a stone cross. The street narrowed at either end to make the collection of market tolls easier. Other business premises lined the street – merchants, drapers, tailors, shoemakers, glovers, weavers, smiths and potters *(25)*. There were butchers stalls or *shammels* and fishmongers at one end so that their noxious smells were isolated as far as possible. Businesses requiring water for power or in the manufacturing process were clustered by the fording places over the two rivers – the corn mill, tanners and a wool 'fulling' or 'tucking' mill. There were no bridges over the rivers and when they were in flood the town was virtually cut off. This made it almost impossible to attend the obligatory mass at the parish church on the hill on Sundays and feast days. However, at the eastern end of the street stood the little chantry chapel of St. James that had served townsfolk and travellers alike for over a hundred years. The chapel belonged to the town and was presided over by a chaplain who was paid from endowments given for mass to be said for the souls of the dead. Hospitality was provided at rest houses and alehouses to the various travellers passing through. These may have been traders, noblemen, soldiers, travelling craftsmen and jobbers; or religious travellers – clergy, monks, nuns and pilgrims. Other occasional visitors included the Bishop and his entourage making a 'visitation' or the assize judges dispensing justice throughout the county on their circuit.

Justice took several forms in the district according to the offenders' status as well as the nature of the offence. There were the quarterly assize courts for more serious crimes, such as murder, serious robbery or rioting. Manorial courts settled disputes over property within the demesne of the manor and there were church courts to oversee adherence to ecclesiastical law. The burgesses – or freemen – of the town had their own courts to deal with petty issues such as using false weights and measures or debts. There was also a special court to deal with any matters, save life or limb, pertaining to *tinners* – that is anyone connected to the digging, processing and selling of alluvial tin from Dartmoor's river valleys. This *stannary* (from the Latin *stannum* for tin) court had its own prison at Lydford which it shared with the court of the Royal Forest of Dartmoor. Punishment and retribution were harsh and swift and usually designed to fit the crime. Lesser crimes might lead to a fine while drunkenness and fighting could land the participants in the stocks. Anyone accused of being a whore might have to suffer the ordeal of being whipped – stripped to the waste and dragged behind a cart from one end of the street to the other and back – while being jeered and pelted with rotten fruit and vegetables. Traders caught short measuring their customers might suffer the indignity of being dunked in the East Okement river by the ducking stool *(26)*. Theft might lead to the amputation of a hand, while murder or treason invariably result in death by hanging or, worse still, being hanged, drawn and quartered. A popular form of summary justice, where suspected adulterers or hen-pecked husbands were concerned, was noisy public ridicule such as having pots and pans banged together outside the their house, all too often at Elizabeth's instigation!

The affairs of the town were governed by the corporate body of burgesses, free from interference from the lords of the castle, as long as due financial recompense was made in lieu of the feudal obligations of service. Robert Courtenay's charter to the burgesses, of some eighty years before, allowed the Burgesses to elect their own *Provost* (or Portreeve) and his assistant, the *Cryer.* It was their job to collect rents and market tolls for the lord but also to oversee and administer the privileges of the Burgesses and the good government of the Borough – *'if a plea relating to the lord arises in the Borough, it ought to be ended within the same'*. Richard Brock had been proud to hold the title of Provost following his election and was steadfast in his negotiations with the late Lord Hugh and his bailiff, Randolph Lecher. Before becoming Provost, he had been actively involved as a burgess in the negotiations to ensure that the town's rights to common pasturage on the lord's wastes and that access to them was protected. The all-important right of pannage for the pigs in the south woods had been exchanged for rights in Hook Wood to the north to make way for his Lordship's new deer park. However, Elizabeth suspected the present Provost, John Fitz John, and his Cryer, John Hare, of being in the lord's pocket and wasn't afraid to voice her opinions in spite of the risk of ending up in the stocks herself.

The Borough had recently had the honour of sending a representative to King Edward's great parliament but in spite of such involvement in wider politics and the comings and goings of travellers along the highway, the town was still very insular and parochial. A regular traveller within the county could recognise where they were simply by listening to the distinctive local dialects of the inhabitants. The town's representation in a national parliament was a rather dubious honour however. The king was making ever-increasing demands on the burgesses' pockets in order to wage war in Scotland, Wales and France and, according to the reports that came back, parliament's main function seemed to be to deliberate on how these taxes should be raised. The ever-growing population, land shortages and increasing wage costs weren't to everyone's advantage either – it was alright if you were a landowner. At least Elizabeth was getting more money and customers for her produce to cover the higher price of flour and her new apprentice's keep. She made sure he earned it however.

Market day was Saturday and peasants travelled in from the surrounding farms, hamlets and villages to sell their stock and produce in the market place. For this privilege they paid a toll of a penny for each beast, a halfpenny for a horse or ox and a penny for five sheep or pigs but nothing for grain. The Provost collected the tolls and received a share for his troubles. Only burgesses of the borough were allowed to buy green hides (untanned skins) or carry on any retail trade and they were exempt from toll throughout the County wherever the Courtenays were lords, including Exeter. For these privileges each burgess paid a shilling (5p) to the lord via the Provost each Michaelmas. Besides holding their acre plots in the town, burgesses also had the grazing rights on the lord's wastes, autumn pannage for their pigs in his woods and, along with the tenants of the manor, common rights upon the King's Forest of Dartmoor. For the latter they had to pay one penny for every beast or twenty sheep at the *drift* (annual round-up) but the rights were a great relief as it spared valuable fodder for the winter months when the weather was too sharp to keep cattle on the moors. Sheep, on the other hand, were capable of withstanding all but the hardest winters on the commons. The working oxen had to be kept inland though as the cultivated land was generally too far from the commons. The arrangement worked well for tenants during good times but, if they were forced to surrender their land or died, the lord was compensated by payment of money or goods in kind. On death, this usually took the form of *herriot* (payment of the best beast), an added blow to the grieving family. If there was no one capable of taking on the tenancy, it often meant destitution.

But today was a happy day when town and country, rich and poor converged on the town for the Festival of St. James. A colourful mixture of entertainment and business was already underway out on the fair field to the south of Fore Street (*27*). There were jesters, musicians and stilt walkers strolling amongst the merchants' stalls, with their exotic wares. Apprentices from the town pitted their strength and guile against farm labourers from the country in a wrestling contest while an archery competition drew a crowd to witness two of the area's finest bowmen battle for supremacy.

After High Mass, a colourful procession left the church, heading back down to the town and to the door of St. James Chapel. It was headed by a group of priests and servers carrying the Holy Cross and a banner bearing an image of the Saint. They wore the scallop shell badges that symbolised him, as did pilgrims travelling to the great Church of Compestella in Spain. The parish priest, William de Winkleigh; Lord Hugh Courtenay's officials, the Provost and Cryer, burgesses and the musicians who accompanied the hymn singing followed them. Lord Hugh himself rode on horseback, accompanied by Lady

Agnes and other members of the household including Lady Eleanor, who was escorted by six nuns and born in a litter due to her advancing age and so as not to look undignified. Elizabeth watched the procession pass with great interest from the front of her shop, feasting her eyes on all the characters and the latest fashions on show – enough material for gossip to last her well into the autumn!

Her eyes fell on poor Hawisia, walking along beside the procession with young Mary, Joanna and Hanna. She looked weary and yet happy to be in the company of her daughters but Elizabeth knew she must be struggling to survive. Despite her reputation, Elizabeth had a warm heart deep down and felt an urge to help her in some way. After greeting her sympathetically she slipped her two fresh loaves and a penny. Hawisia looked embarrassed and yet was too needy to refuse the charity. At that moment Lady Eleanor passed and glimpsed across to were they both stood. Almost at once there seemed to be a sub-conscious recognition of the common bond the three of them shared and of how their respective destinies were somehow linked. For, in spite of the enormous social divisions between them, they were each dependent on the other in one way or another.

PLAGUE, BLOODSHED AND CHANGE

The early decades of the fourteenth century brought mixed fortunes to our three widows and their families. Sadly, poor Hawisia died herself – from a combination of malnutrition, prolonged smoke inhalation and sheer exhaustion – before her hopes of finding a secure home and suitable husbands for her daughters could be realised. However, the younger daughters were taken in by her cousin, a tenant in the neighbouring parish of Belstone and barely a stones throw from Byrham. They went on to marry his two sons and bore many children between them. Mary, on the other hand, never married and remained a faithful maidservant to the Courtenay family for the rest of her life. Lady Eleanor lived to a ripe old age, dying in London on 30th September 1328, but not long enough to witness her son finally obtaining the title of Earl of Devon from King Edward III in 1335. He had become active in national politics, including fierce opposition to King Edward II. Five years after finally obtaining the Earldom, both he and Agnes died. They were buried together amid great pomp and ceremony in Cowick Priory. Their eldest son, John, did indeed obtain a prominent place in the church, becoming Abbot of Tavistock Abbey in 1334. His younger brother, Hugh, succeeded to the Earldom and the Courtenay estates on his father's death and married Margaret de Bohun, granddaughter of King Edward I. Powderham Castle passed to the Courtenay family as dowry. This was to become the family's principal residence right down to the present day. Hugh III became one of the original Knights of the Garter and was buried in Exeter Cathedral in 1377. He and Margaret had no less than nine daughters and eight sons and William, their fourth son, achieved the highest rank in the medieval English Catholic Church as the Archbishop of Canterbury. Meanwhile, Elizabeth Brock had the satisfaction of seeing her nephew marry and produce an heir – delivered by her own hands of course! The business prospered and Brocks were to remain prominent in town business and affairs well into the twentieth century.

The Courtenay's deer park became firmly established against the moor's edge. Vestiges of the parkland boundaries, the abandoned settlements, the probable remains of the hunting lodge (*28*) and even ancient holly and hawthorn trees that may well have been introduced as coverts for the deer centuries before, can still be clearly seen in the landscape today. Place names provide further evidence – Old Park, Kennel Field and My Lord's Field – the latter possibly being where fodder was produced to sustain the deer through the harsh winters. The deer would most likely have been roe deer – especially introduced –

numerous bones uncovered during excavations at the castle provide evidence of this. Native red deer would also have been seen (and may still be seen in the old park occasionally) but these were the preserves of royalty. Care would have been taken to contain the Courtenay deer within the park but gates were provided to enable them to be turned out into the larger 'chase' (consisting of much of the greater parish of Okehampton) when required. It was also important to separate the deer herd from those of the Crown on the adjoining Royal Forest of Dartmoor and to keep them from entering the surrounding arable land. This was achieved by natural boundaries formed by the rivers or substantial walls and ditches called 'deer leaps'. These were constructed with banks and ditches to enable deer to jump over one way but not the other. Such boundaries didn't keep poachers out however and in one recorded incident of the early fourteenthth century, the Rectors of Broadwoodwidger and Tedburn St. Mary no less, were caught poaching and, when challenged, proceeded to assault the park keepers! There were fishponds in the park also, probably near the castle. Although their exact location is not known, they were later referred to in leases of the seventeenth and eighteenth centuries.

Ever-increasing traffic along the old highway passing through Okehampton brought yet more trade. While much of Europe and the eastern parts of England suffered a succession of terrible summers and poor harvests in the first half of the century, the west of England seems to have escaped more lightly and may even have profited from others' misfortune. Fortunes were soon to change for the worse for everyone however when a new and deadly threat appeared on the horizon – the Black Death. Neighbouring Dorset was the first county to experience the terror of the bubonic plague (29). Merchants, bringing expensive spices and fine silks from the Far East to an eager western market, unwittingly carried a more sinister cargo aboard their rat-infested ships. Although not recognised at the time, it was the fleas, which fed off the rats, that were responsible for the spread of the plague. From its introduction to this country by men fleeing from France to Melcome Regis in Dorset in 1348, it spread to all parts of the country in the space of barely a year. The plague was no respecter of wealth or station and affected both rich and poor, priest and sinner. Almost half of Devon's clergy perished between 1349 and 1351 and Okehampton had no less than five different priests during this period – even their prayers could not save them. Many people no doubt turned to the age-old belief in the curative powers of ancient springs and Holy wells and sought the help of the saints to which many of them were dedicated. An old spring which formerly emerged from the bank at the junction of High Street and Church

Lane was known as Rock Well before it was covered and piped under the road to the river just below West Bridge in the 1900s. St. Roche, who lived in France in the early fourtewenth century, was supposedly imbued with powers against the plague and was inevitably called upon a great deal at this time. Could there be a link? It is tempting to speculate whether this was once St. Roche's well in the days before the Protestant reformation movement attempted to sweep such 'superstitious' associations away.

The plague was real enough however. In all some 2,500,000 people – half the population – died across the whole country. In 1377, the total population of Devon stood at around 75,000 – less than the estimated population at the time of the Domesday Survey nearly 300 years before. The situation in Okehampton must have been much the same. Although the population was to grow again steadily, a succession of plagues continued to revisit Okehampton down the generations, bringing untold misery to the population of both town and country. Aside from the human tragedy, the Black Death brought about a great shortage of labour and resulted in vast areas of land and many settlements being abandoned. For the survivors this meant opportunity though. The old feudal system began to break down and money became more widely circulated. Wages for labourers increased considerably and the holdings of many free tenants expanded, making them more viable and, ultimately, gave rise to the steadfast yeomanry of Elizabethan Devon.

Many churches, including Okehampton's, were re-built during this period in the ubiquitous Perpendicular style with gilded rood screens, dividing the nave from the chancel, finely carved bench ends and colourful, symbolic bosses adorning the elaborate barrel roofs. Stained glass windows and the painted panels of the rood screen bore images of numerous Saints and the plastered interior walls were painted with depictions of biblical stories and popular moral tales, such as St. George and the Dragon, representing the triumph of good over evil. At Okehampton there would have been two altars – one to Our Lady, bearing the image of the Virgin Mary, and another to St. John. Other trappings of the Roman Catholic faith would have included incense burners, a large candlestick carrying twenty five candles, the pyx containing the blessed sacrament, a pax pole for the kiss of peace and a large cross which was carried in processions on festival days. Newly-cast bells called parishioners to divine service from the numerous substantial stone towers that from thence forward clearly marked the position of towns and villages in the landscape. The skills and sheer degree of labour required to build and maintain these magnificent buildings must have created continuous employment for many people in the district.

The church was the focus of community life, with both secular and religious activities taking place within and so gifts towards such 'great works' were plentiful. Such gifts were also considered a means of buying a place in Heaven. John Newecum, who was Vicar of Okehampton between 1413 and 1451, was behind the re-building of All Saints in 1447, following a dispute with the prior and monks of Cowick Priory. There were two aisles, the one on the north side known as the Kigbeare Aisle as the parishioners from that hamlet maintained it. Sadly, only the tower and the piers of the arcade of this church survives however after a disastrous fire destroyed much of the nave and chancel in 1842, after which they were completely re-built, roughly to the same plan. In addition to gifts, there was income from tithes and the commercial activities of the churchwardens or 'stores' who were charged with deriving income for the upkeep of the parish church and welfare provision. Money was raised from sales of ale, brewed especially for church purposes, trade in sheep and wool and, in some parishes, active involvement in the production, processing and selling of tin (the *stannary* – 'tinners' centre' – of Chagford for instance). The annual festivals were traditionally times of giving. An area of the nave was often set aside for the ever-popular 'miracle plays' or they were performed in the market place. In Okehampton's case, festivities were organised by the parish's Wardens of the Summer Plays and the Hoganers. The latter were responsible for the sports at Hocktide (the second Monday and Tuesday after Easter). This probably included the old custom of *hocking* where first girls and then boys had to try and catch a member of the opposite sex. Those caught would then have to pay a forfeit to the church, thus bolstering the parish coffers as well as providing an excellent opportunity for flirting with the full blessing of the church!

In 1365 the townspeople petitioned Pope Urban V for permission to celebrate divine service in St. James Chapel in place of the parish church. They pleaded that they were 'between two streams of water, on account of which floods often occur, so that for the distance of a mile or so it is impossible to hear divine service'. They also pointed out that they needed to provide for travellers along the highway through the town 'by which many caravans enter and pass'. It was probably soon after this that the chapel was re-built. This may well have been at the instigation of Dame Joan Courtenay who endowed it with land for two priests so that they could say masses for her brother's soul. Once again, only the tower of this building remains as the nave was re-built in 1862. The original nave was slightly smaller than the present one and, by the eighteenth century, was hemmed-in by houses. Three were built against its walls and leased out by the Wardens in order to provide income for its upkeep *(30)*.

The wool trade continued to flourish in the district, with the Dartmoor commons providing ample grazing for the sheep. The fast flowing, clear streams coming off the moor providing water for to power the fulling mills and was also used in the washing operations. Coarse serge cloth remained the principal output of the industry in the west of the county, while finer 'kerseys' were produced on the eastern side of Dartmoor, and in mid and east Devon. Apart from the mills, most of the processes – carding, spinning and weaving – took place in people's homes or above their shops. Another source of income at this time would have been tin working in the vicinity. The Devon Stannary (tin mining administrative region) was divided up into four districts, each with a stannary town as its centre – Chagford, Tavistock, Plympton and Ashburton. Here tinners' courts were held and the smelted or 'white' tin was taken to be weighed and *coigned* (a small piece trimmed off for assaying to test for purity) by Crown officials so that taxes could be levied. Twenty-four Stannators were elected to represent each district at the great court or parliament each year. This originally met in the open air at Crockern Tor in the centre of Dartmoor. The 'parliament' had extraordinary privileges for the time – encouraged by the Crown, who benefited from the taxes levied of course. Anyone could claim to be a tinner and thus free from all other courts and obligations, provided they registered the 'bonds' (claims) with the stannary courts and produced tin within the year. These bounds could be laid virtually anywhere, regardless of ownership. Merchants and shareholders in tin works could also claim tinners' rights. Inevitably this led to abuses as well as freedoms and the stannary courthouse and prison at Lydford gained a particularly bad reputation for rough justice as people who offended the tinners down the centuries were to find to their cost!

Okehampton's tinners fell under the jurisdiction of the Chagford court. In fact, the Churchwardens of that town were particularly active in tin workings in the district including one known as 'Bubhill' or 'Skit'. The old excavations can still be seen up the valley from East Okement (formerly Harter) Farm on the East Okement river. Others can be found on the Black-a-ven-Brook, on the East Okement above Fatherford viaduct *(31)* and on the higher reaches of the West Okement and its tributary, the Red-a-ven Brook . These 'stream works' were developed to extract the alluvial cassiterite (tin) from the gravels of the river valleys where they had been washed from lodes higher up. By diverting the course of the streams, tinners were able to wash over the gravels and settle-out the heavier tin ore in wooden troughs or *buddles*. The ore was then taken to a 'stamping mill' and placed on a flat stone beneath a set of two or three metal-tipped vertical wooden beams or 'stamps'. These were lifted in turn by cams on a water-powered shaft and dropped onto the tin ore, thus crushing it to fine gravel. The ore was then further refined through buddles before being smelted in a small, clay-lined furnace in a *blowing house*. The required temperature was achieved by blowing air into the furnace from a set of wood and leather bellows, again worked by a water wheel. Examples of the remains of these mills can be found all over Dartmoor, including the Taw and West Okement valleys (*32*).

Another subsidiary industry would have been coppicing and charcoal burning as the blowing houses required vast quantities of charcoal to smelt the ore produced. Forestry workers generally must have been in demand with timber required for building, hazel and ash for hurdle making, bark for leather tanning and so on. Then, of course, there would have been the tradespeople required to service the farms and other businesses – blacksmiths, carpenters, coopers and wheelwrights. However, wheeled vehicles were far from commonplace. The state of the roads and tracks and the hilly nature of the moorland edge meant that packhorses and ox-drawn sledges were more often seen. Then there were house builders and thatchers, not to mention general labourers and 'jobbers' – travelling labourers and farmhands who took up seasonal employment where and when required – and those 'in-service'.

Away from the hustle and bustle of everyday life in the town and district in the late fifteenth century, very different lives were being played out in the homes of the most powerful and influential families in the land. During their infrequent stays at the Castle, the Courtenays were to spend much of their time in preparations for the latest hostilities in the 'Wars of the Roses'. During a very active life, Thomas Courtenay, the 5th Earl of Devon, was a ward of King Henry VI, married Margaret, the daughter of the first Earl of Somerset, quarrelled with the Earl of Arundel, fought with Lord Bonville and pillaged Exeter Cathedral. He initially fought for the Yorkist cause but, having been impeached for treason in 1454, obtained a pardon and eventually died in 1458 while in attendance on the King. His son, Thomas, the 6th Earl, fought for King Henry VI at Northampton and Wakefield in 1460 but was captured at Towton the following year and beheaded. Okehampton and the other estates were briefly forfeited to King Edward IV until Henry's return to the throne when they were restored to Thomas's son, John, who was killed at the battle of Tewkesbury in 1471. Various other members of the family were either killed in battle or beheaded. Eventually the Earldom was restored to Edward Courtenay, grandson of Sir

Hugh Courtenay of Haccombe and Boconoc, who was brother to Edward Courtenay, 3rd Earl of Devon – known as 'the Blind Earl'.

For a while the Courtenays seemed to be in favour with the Crown again. Indeed William, the 8th Earl, even married Katherine, daughter of King Edward IV, but was later imprisoned in the Tower of London, together with his son and grandson. He was released by King Henry VIII on his accession to the throne and the Earldom was restored once again. Sadly, William died just before the investiture however but the King allowed him to be buried as an Earl. His son, Henry, the 9th Earl attained the greatest status of any in the family before him when King Henry VIII created him Marquis of Exeter. At first the two men were great friends, perhaps too close, for the King's sense of insecurity led him to accuse the Marquis of entering a conspiracy with Cardinal Pole. He was attainted and beheaded on the 9th January 1539. With him ended the family's long association with Okehampton Castle as a great residence. The estates were once again confiscated and the great hunting park abandoned. Despite no charge being levelled against him, the Marquis's son, Edward, was sent to the Tower where he remained until the accession of Queen Mary. The Earldom was restored yet again and it was even suggested that he might marry the Queen but, as had been the case for so many of his ancestors, fortune turned against him and he was exiled to Padua where he died in 1556.

The estates were then divided among the descendants of the four sisters of Edward Courtenay, the 7th Earl – the Arundells, Trethurffes, Mohuns, Vivians, Bullers and Trelawnys. Meanwhile, the good burgesses of Okehampton, ever mindful of any opportunity to strengthen their position, commenced the long and expensive business of purchasing the rights to the borough and market from these families. As for the castle itself, well, it was a shame to leave all that lead, glass and dressed stone to go to waste! Even today fragments of worked stone can be found in buildings around the town. The old park became woodland and pasture, with new enclosures being laid out within during the eighteenth century.

The hard lessons learned by the Courtenays seem not to have influenced their former subjects however, for soon it was the ordinary townspeople and neighbouring villagers who were to experience the fear and bloodshed of battle first hand as they got too close to affairs of church and state. People had already witnessed Henry VIII's suppression of the chantries and the dissolution of the monasteries, Tavistock included. A new 'middle class' was rising to take the place of the noble families who were virtually wiped out in the turmoil of the royal feuding of the previous century. They also profited from the downfall of the great religious houses. The Russells (later Dukes of Bedford) for instance obtained the Tavistock Abbey lands and rights, and, along with them, the advowson (right to tithes) of Okehampton parish which had been conferred on the Abbey by King Edward IV. Now Edward was introducing sweeping changes to the Catholic Church in England. All images and altars were removed, by order, from the churches and members of the clergy were allowed to marry. These changes were resented by many in this conservative corner of the country and the final straw came with the introduction of the English Prayer Book, in place of the familiar Latin order of service, in 1549.

When the parishioners of neighbouring Sampford Courtenay heard the new service on Whit-Monday morning they didn't like it. Even though few of them could read or write, let alone understand the Latin chants of the old service, it was one change too many. They forced the priest to say mass in the old style and gathered in protest outside after. A local gentleman, named William Hellyons, tactlessly remonstrated with the restless crowd and paid with his life. He was first struck on the neck with a billhook by a farmer named Lethbridge and then hacked to death by the mob on the steps of the Church House. From then on there was no turning back. The angry villagers, led by a tailor called Underhill, marched on Exeter, joining up with other rebels on the way, including many from Cornwall who had risen independently. After a skirmish at Crediton, they arrived at the gates to Exeter where, in spite of having the sympathy of many within the walls, they were kept at bay. The city was surrounded, besieged and bombarded. The West Gate was nearly taken before Edward Seymour, "Protector" Somerset, intervened by dispatching Lord Russell with a Royal army, bolstered by Italian, German and Welsh mercenaries. The rebels consisted mostly of ill-equipped peasants and were no match for the trained soldiers of Lord Russell's army. Nevertheless they put up a brave fight and no less than five bloody battles ensued, starting at Fenny Bridges. There were skirmishes in the streets of Okehampton too before the rebels re-grouped for one last desperate stand back in the streets of Sampford Courtenay. One account claims that over 800 died in this battle alone. The reckoning that followed was no less bloody, with those who escaped the battles with their lives being tracked down and summarily executed. One Exeter priest was reportedly hung from his own tower as a grisly reminder to the citizens of the futility of their opposition to the changes. God rest their souls.

Physical changes to the places of worship were soon to follow as all the outward symbols of Roman Catholicism were removed and, in spite of such desperate resistance, within a generation or two the old religion was largely forgotten. By the beginning of the seventeenth century, things were changing for the better in Okehampton – in terms of trade and the economy at least. The burgesses were endeavouring to obtain all the rights needed to give them the collective freedom and individual commercial advantage they desired. In a series of expensive deals and messy law suits, they eventually succeeded in this aim and, in the process, obtained a Charter of Incorporation from King James I in 1623, as a means of strengthening their claims. As before, the Charter restricted the right to carry on retail trade or handicrafts to freemen of the borough, except under special licence or at markets and fairs. It defined the borough boundary as encompassing a half-mile radius of the market cross in the town's centre and created a corporation consisting of a mayor, seven principal burgesses and eight assistant burgesses to govern its affairs. These appointments were to be for life with any vacancies filled by the Council itself. For legal reasons however, it was necessary to retain the office of Portreeve in order to collect market tolls and the position was generally filled by the incoming mayor soon after his election each year at Michaelmas.

Those charged with assisting the Corporation to look after the administration of justice and the town's finances and legal affairs were to include a Recorder, Justice and Town Clerk, in turn assisted by two Sergeants at mace and two Constables. There was also a Receiver who gathered rents and tolls and fulfilled the role of a borough surveyor – maintaining the roads, bridges and water sources within the borough. He was assisted in this role by a Scavenger who helped keep the streets clean and carried out market duties. The borough's Chaplain of St. James Chapel also acted as Master of the small Grammar School near the West Bridge where he taught Latin to six or eight boys nominated by the Mayor and Corporation plus as many fee paying boarders from better-off families. There was a small pound by the chapel where the inhabitants' pigs would be driven by the Scavenger if they strayed and, not far away, the modest 'Guildhall' where borough affairs were conducted before the present Town Hall was converted for the purpose in 1826. Borough property was not inconsiderable though and included Westacott Farm in the neighbouring parish of Inwardleigh and Maddaford in Kigbeare hamlet among some thirty 'Ancient Town Lands' and another forty holdings classified as 'Borough Lands'. Another dozen were held jointly for the benefit of the borough and the parish through the vicar and churchwardens. Between them, these properties provided a considerable annual income to support the growing town bureaucracy

The new Corporation was given legal powers also. A borough court of record was established and given authority to try any case involving an offence within the borough where the punishment was not likely to involve loss of life or limb and to deal with any pleas under £30. A court of *pie-poudre* was also granted whereby petty offences, in connection with the fairs and markets, could be dealt with speedily. As always though, justice tended to be swift and often harsh or humiliating. Only the more serious crimes were held over until the next quarter sessions. Punishments ranged from a fine – or a few hours in the stocks for those who could not afford to pay – to whipping, a dip in the ducking stool or imprisonment. In spite of such deterrents and a growing 'puritan' element among the town's leaders, Okehampton was still a fairly lawless place in the seventeenth century according to the records however.

It is from this period that the infamous association with Lady Howard comes. According to local legend she murdered three of her four husbands as well as two of her children. Her penance is to travel nightly from her father's house at Fitzford, Tavistock to the castle grounds where she has to pick a blade of grass and take it home. Only when she has succeeded in removing every blade, or the world comes to an end, will the task be complete and her soul rest in peace. On moon-lit nights it is said that she can be seen riding in her coach, made of her victims' bones and surmounted with a skull at the apex and one at each corner. It rattles through the streets of Tavistock and along the old King Way over the moors to Okehampton, driven by a headless horseman and pulled by four horses, preceded by a large spectral black hound with a single glaring eye in the centre of its forehead. One early recorded version of the legend refers only to her spirit taking the form of a black dog, while another refers to her riding in a coach of bones but it seems that the story has been embellished by various tellers and writers down the years. The great folklorist 'squarson' of Lewtrenchard, Sabine Baring-Gould recorded a ballad at the turn of the twentieth century which ran:–

> *My Ladye hath a sable coach*
> *With horses two and four*
> *My Ladye hath a gaunt blood-hound*
> *That goeth on before.*
> *My Ladye's coach hath nodding plumes*
> *The driver hath no head.*
> *My Ladye is an ashen white*
> *As one who is long dead.*

In fact, there is no historical basis to the crimes she supposedly committed and her character has clearly been unjustly maligned down the centuries. Lady

Mary Howard was the daughter of Sir John Fitz who certainly was no saint. He was allegedly responsible for at least two murders while under the influence of drink and eventually stabbed himself to death in 1605. Her mother was Gertrude Courtenay of Landrake, a descendent of Lady Elizabeth Courtenay, great aunt to Lord Edward and a co-heiress to the family estates (hence the connection with the castle). She was a woman of noted beauty and charm. Mary Fitz, their only daughter, was born in 1596 and, although inheriting her father's fortune, she seems to have inherited more of her mother's characteristics. Naturally, this must have made her an attractive match and she proceeded to marry in turn: Sir Alan Percy, Knight; Thomas Darcy, Esq.; Sir Charles Howard (brother of the Earl of Suffolk) and Sir Richard Grenville, Bart. She was only sixteen when she married for the third time and, though not accumulating any substantial extra wealth through her first three marriages, she was worth a considerable amount in her own right by the time she met her last husband around the mid 1620s. She apparently also retained much of her beauty as she was only in her early thirties then. Which quality attracted Sir Richard most is not recorded but, either way, he shortly became dissatisfied and indifferent towards her and treated her so badly that she ended up divorcing him in around 1633 and going to live with her late husband's family while reverting back to her former name. Sir Richard was not too concerned by this until he discovered that she had made a pre-marital conveyance of her entire fortune to the Earl of Suffolk who duly took possession of the property. He subsequently lost a lawsuit against the Earl and ended up in prison for speaking slanderously of him. During the Civil War he became the King's General in the West though and obtained a royal warrant ordering the reinstatement of his wife's property to him on the grounds that she was backing Parliament. She eventually died at Fitzford House in 1671. Perhaps it was he who instigated the myth of his former wife's ill-doings as revenge. Perhaps historians have simply mixed her deeds up with those of her father or her namesake, Lady Frances Howard of the court of James I, who was indeed sent to the Tower for poisoning two of her four husbands. Or, maybe, incidental references to a headless horseman, a white lady, skulls and a whisht hound were drawn from much older legendary associations with the site? We shall never know but, even now, a walk by the castle ruins by the glint of the moon is not an experience for the faint-of-heart!

CHRONICLES OF A TURBULENT TIME

The year was 1625 and John Rattenbury (*33*) sat in his parlour, with quill pen poised and contemplated the first entry in his new journal. He had just had the honour of being appointed Town Clerk to the newly incorporated Borough of Okehampton. He seemed the ideal choice given his family's long association with the town and a sound knowledge of the law gained through his training as an attorney. His father was *Escheator* (*34*) for Devon and Cornwall and his brother, Peter, was also involved in the affairs of the Borough. John was small in stature but had a certain presence about him. He dressed as a puritan but the pince-nais spectacles perched on the end of his nose gave him a learned air. He lived in a prominent house, fronting Fore Street on the northern, sunny side. It was timber framed and three stories in height – far more substantial and imposing than most of the town houses which were still largely constructed of cob and thatch. Heavy wainscoting (wood panelling) distinguished it on the inside and reflected his status as one of the 'chiefest inhabitants' of the borough. In spite of his status and relative wealth, his possessions were still

View of Okehampton from the south in the late 17th century from 'The Travels of Cosmo III, Grand Duke of Tuscany in the reign of Charles II', reproduced by J. Mawman in 1821. The view was drawn from the area of modern Station Road and shows how most of the houses lay along the main road from High Street and the parish church to the left to St. James Chapel on the right. The distinctive gabled roof of Northmore House (now the Town Hall) can be seen slightly left of the centre, with the road to Hatherleigh stretching away behind. (Museum of Dartmoor Life)

This unsigned watercolour of West Bridge in the mid 19th century shows the old town gaol on the far side and the London Inn on the right with the Methodist church (built 1841) beyond. (Museum of Dartmoor Life)

fairly modest however. His parlour was furnished with a table, settle, chair, a number of stools and a servant's *trundle bed* (a low wheeled bed); the hall with a table, bench, cupboard and two chairs. Smaller items included, a bed-warming pan, pewter tableware, cutlery, cooking pots and pans and, of course, his beloved books (35). The windows were glazed, unlike the majority of houses in the neighbourhood although the curtains of the four poster bed were still essential to exclude draughts. An oak chest or *coffer* contained blankets and family valuables including John's treasured Bible.

The town still consisted basically of one long main street but the stalls or *shambles* down the middle of the medieval market place in the centre had been progressively built up into two rows of cottages and shops at either end of the main street. There was an open square about half way along known as the Parade where the ancient market cross still stood at the centre of the borough. The burgage plots stretching back to the river to the north of Fore Street, still survived more or less in tact. Many of those to the south had been filled in as courtyards containing a mixture of cottages and workshops with gangways leading off the Back Street to the south of Middle Row. The old Guildhall stood in the eastern Middle Row that stretched from the Parade right up to the door of St. James Chapel. The houses built up against its north wall and a pig pound to the northeast now hemmed this in. A curfew (*36*) bell hung from the tower of the chapel and was rung every evening at eight o'clock as a signal to the inhabitants to extinguish their fires in order to reduce the risk of fire among the thatched roofs and ricks of faggots and furze. To the east stood the hump-backed East Bridge. On the lower side of this was a dipping place, where townsfolk went for water, but it was also the home of the infamous ducking stool. At the other end of the town a little back lane, to the north of the western Middle Row, ran down to another dipping place near the old West Quay. The foot ferry that had once conveyed travellers and townsfolk attending the parish church had ceased to operate, having been superseded by the new West Bridge upstream – also hump-backed. Below this was the town pound for stray animals beside the weir which turned water into the leat (water course) supplying the water wheel of a corn mill a short way down stream. Nearby stood the schoolmaster's house and the little grammar school. The schoolroom on the upper floor of the small thatched building was reached by a flight of steps against the wall. On the higher side of the bridge stood the cottage, which the new Corporation had converted into a prison and accommodation for a gaol keeper, at a cost of £40.

An early 19th century sketch of Back Street showing Middle Row and the old Guildhall on the left with the steep pitched roof of Mount Ribbon attached to the tower of St. James beyond. The hanging sign to the right is that of the former New Inn. (Museum of Dartmoor Life)

The principal occupations of the inhabitants of the town and surrounding parish revolved mainly around farming and related trades such as milling, spinning and weaving, tanning, boot and glove making. Many of the open areas around the town were filled with drying racks on which the freshly woven and *fulled* (37) serges were stretched to dry. On market days the streets were crowded with stalls on trestles or *standings*, rented out by the Corporation and stored under the Guildhall. The butchers set up their flesh shambles in Back Street where there was more shade but they still tended to attract many flies and, inevitably, dogs. Produce and livestock brought to the market included sheep and cattle, cheeses of high repute, wheat, barley and oats. The latter were not so highly renowned – as one observer put it "The oats which they sow be all spoiled oats and the drink that they do make thereof spoiled drink... what creature so ever do eat or taste thereof it will make him vomit!". Nevertheless, there were several inns and alehouses to cater for travellers and the 'lower orders' amongst the townsfolk. Ale and cider no doubt took their mind off their wretched state but was more often than not the cause of it in John's opinion. Craftsmen commonly earned a shilling (5p) a day and labourers sixpence (2.5p). A quart (1 litre) of strong beer cost a penny (0.5p) by comparison. A fine for drunkenness, on the other hand, would set a man back five shillings (25p) so it was not difficult to get on the slippery slope to destitution.

Although John was generally liberal-minded, in religious matters he had a leaning towards the puritanical views of some of his colleagues on the Corporation and endeavoured to uphold good Christian principals in his dealings and to set a good example to others. He was particularly proud to attend quarter sessions with the rest of the Corporation 'in state'. At the same time though, he had a compassionate nature and thus did not support some of the more bigoted views of his friends. He was certainly no lover of the old Catholic religion and the occasional attempts to re-introduce some of the old 'Papist' ways, though in fact it was hard to believe that in his great grandfather's time, a little over three quarters of a century before, men had laid down their lives in the district in defence of such practices. Although the great monasteries had been dissolved beyond living memory and now either lay in ruins or had been put to secular use, bishops and other members of the old church hierarchy had been retained. There was a deep-seated resentment in dealings between the church and the now staunchly protestant Corporation which would rankle for many years.

John's pride in the independence and achievements of the new Corporation meant that he was keen to chronicle the successes of the burgesses and any notable events in the town. After all, he was one of the privileged few who could read or write – even among the other 'chiefest inhabitants'. Rudimentary education in Latin letters had been available to a few of the town's boys for some years and the new Corporation recognised the benefits of providing such education for the general betterment of the town. As few had the means to pay for their sons to attend however, the Mayor would nominate half a dozen or so boys each year for a scholarship from the income of the generous bequest of Master Harragroe (*38*). The schoolmaster was paid £12 per annum for his duties 'being the gift of the corporation for his better encouragement' and was also permitted to take fee-paying borders. One of the first priorities however had to be law and order. Ignorance, squalor and lack of opportunities didn't help of course but, John believed strongly that if all men were 'pious to God, loyal to the King and loved one another', the town would be a better place. As it was, the only way of dealing with drunkenness and non-attendance at church was to punish the offenders. Perhaps the new prison would act as a visible reminder on earth of the eternal punishment to come in the hereafter.

John's brother, Peter, had been sworn in as Mayor the previous October and in April, King James's son, Charles I, had been proclaimed King of England, Scotland and France. John recorded these events in his journal with pride and hoped for peace and prosperity under Charles but the new King and the old enemy from across the water had other ideas.

5 Sept. 1625. King Charles came to plimouth, and stayd 8 dayes att wch time John Glanvill Esqr Recorder of this towne wa[s] commanded by the King to goe a voyage in warfare as Secretary to the Councell of warre, Viz to C[ales].

At least this warfare was a long way off but that other old enemy, the plague, still visited the town at intervals and his next entry was a painful one but also reflected his relief that his immediate family were not affected and that law and order had been maintained.

This yeare there was a very great Sicknesse and Visitation of the pestilence in this towne whereof dyed about 300 people most of them of the younger sort & from Easter Even 1626 untill after Michaelmas following, noe markett att all Kept here save only some small quantity of victualls brought in weekly on the markett day by 2 or 3 Butchers of this towne and parish dureing all of wch time most part the Inhabitants (nott being permitted to travell abroade Except only to the Citty of Exon [Exeter] upon Mr Mayors certificate of being Free &c) made there aboade & continued here & noe Taxe or Rates for Releife being had from others places (as most of [the] other townes now visited had) by the procurement & Letters, of the Mayor, Justice and some of the principall Burgesses there was some voluntury benevolence from divers parishes & persons brough[t] in amounting to 55" [£55] odd mony & some provision of Corne and Victualls sent alsoe & the same from tyme to tyme by the Mayor & his appointement, distribarded & bestowed for the Releif of the poore he[re] inhabiting as by the booke of perticulers thereof written out since by the towne clerke may appear, dureing all wch time by the providence of Almighty god & the great paines & especiall Care of the mayor and Justice the sick people were from time to time releived wch necessaryes the often intended disorders and outrages quietly repressed and appeased & noe hurt losse or Violent damage of any value done to any person, whatsoever, god bee thanked for itt.

His heart was heavy as he referred to the 'younger sort' as he recalled those he used to talk with and a couple of promising scholars at the Grammar School. He remembered with a smile their muddy but determined faces during the *spurling* (the custom of scrabbling for apples in a miry place) on the last occasion that the parish bounds were beat. Now, so many of those with whom the town's future lay, were gone. Later that year, John had added honour of being elected Mayor himself and recorded with pride:

Johes [John] Rattenbury gent elcus Major 2d die Octobris, 1626.

This Yeare the Mayor & principall Burgesses seate, & the Assistants seate in the Church were sett up there. And New Seates made & sett Up in the Chaple att the Cost of the Corporacon. This Yeare the loft for the Organs in the Church & for the seates there wth the new windowe in the Roughe were finished & the Organs repayred.

Such improvements and the dignified procession of the burgesses to the chapel at the quarter sessions were all designed to reflect the new status of the borough and Corporation.

1627, This yeare, from the 20th November, until the 18th of January, the Mayor officers & inhabitants were much troubled & charged by the Soldiers billited here & the Charg of many sick Soldiers left unpayd.

He wrote this entry with some indignation as, in spite of his loyalty to the King, the imposition was a rather unwelcome one and such demands were increasingly being made on towns without recourse to Parliament. It was the haughty attitude of the officers rather than the good King himself that offended him most however. The following year saw the Petition of Rights presented to His Majesty by Parliament and the King agreed not to make further demands of this nature or levy taxes without first seeking Parliament's approval.

3 August 1628, being sabboth day. About 4 of the Clocke in the afternoone ymediately after Evening prayer ended att the Church of Okehampton there being noe rayne perceaved to fall wth in or neare this towne & the streetes then very drye, the water here called Lede, or the East water was suddenly risen about some v. foote at the Easte bridge, running at a more Violent manner than had beene usually knowne & twas conceived the water did savour & smell of some brimstone.

A most curious incident that caused some unease amongst the congregation - the work of the devil maybe? For these were superstitious times and accusations of witchcraft were rife.

1628, This year the Moytie of the borough of Okehampton was purchased of the Right honor'ble John Lord Mohun Baron of Okehampton for which was payd, CC" [£200] & an yearly Rent Charge of xii" [£12] in ffee.

John winced a little as he considered the high cost of purchasing this further share of the rights to the borough, the Baron had certainly driven a hard bargain! There was only one more share to acquire and the town's aspirations would be met. His personal ambition received a boost with his appointment as Escheator for Devon and Cornwall in 1628 following his brother's term from 1626 and his father's last term of 1624 – a real family affair!

He was immensely proud of his family's success, grateful for his own good fortune and ever mindful that there were people a lot worse off.

It was ordered & agreed this yeare that wth the profitt to be yearely raysed of the forty pounds given by Captain Bickle two of the poorest men & two of the poorest women here shoulde have Each a cloth gowne yearely at Christmas.

He couldn't help believing that at least some of this poverty was caused by un-Godly conduct however. His brother was again elected Mayor in 1629 and it came as rather a shock when he found his own kin on the wrong side of the law.

6th Aprill [1630] The Mayor arrested by the Sherriffs Bayliffs [as] he was Coming from the Sessions at the Town ha[ll] in an action of Battery brought against him [&] georg Crocker one of the Con'bles att the suit of John Wood gent.

This is hardly the example he would have wished to see projected by the chiefest inhabitants, let alone his own brother. Nevertheless, the Corporation was anxious to set a good example and to offer suitable instruction and encouragement to townsfolk in leading a God-fearing life rather than having to resort to the law. But first they had to persuade those who needed the instruction most to attend church in the first place. John was elected Mayor once again and was determined to see law and order firmly established in the borough.

The Legacy of 50" [£50] given by Georg Cottle gent imployed by 4" [£4] payd unto the Churchwardens & bestowed by them in bread weekly brought to the parish Church of Okehampton Viz, xiij pennyworth & there after morning prayer & Sermon Ended distributed to the poorest people & for the Sermon on St Georges day x" [£10], residue spent at a dinner on such as were present at that Sermon as by his will.

December [1632]. The lecture at the chapel appointed & began upon the town court days, by Mr. Michael Porter.

John was hopeful that the instruction from these sermons would serve their purpose but his hopes were frustrated and the lectures apparently fell on deaf ears.

1633. Sundry misdemenors Vz of Drunkards Swearers & gamsters &c Questioned presented & punished this year of the penalties of which the some of Three pounds & fifteen Shillings &c distributed & given to the poore by Wm. Drew & Robert Brock Constables here this yeare.

August 26 [1635]. Thomas Reddaway comitted to prison for abusing the Mayor Until &c after bound to the good behauiour And Entered into Recognizance not to play at Unlawf[ul] games nor to haunt any such places.

Divers Misdimenors of Ddrunkard(s) Swearers gamsters & others punished this yeare. And the penalties Levied distributed to ye poore.

March 31, 1636. Roger Oake sent to the gaole at Exter for stabbing & killing William Slade & afterwards Executed.

Edmund Can the Elder for speaking slanderously against the government of this towne was committed &c bound to his good behaviour. And payd 5" [£5] for being drunke.

Mr. Cann had had the audacity to say that the town had 'lately been governed by a company of knaves!' Perhaps perseverance would pay off. At least the Mayor and burgesses hadn't been troubled by unruly soldiers of late, nor been faced with any other unfair demands on the town's purse since Parliament's stand against the King on the matter, even though he had dismissed them the following year. The Royal Navy was being re-built after several years of neglect following the great victory over the Spanish Armada of half a century before. This was costing taxpayers a great deal of money, but was a matter for the coastal towns who benefited from the navy's protection. Okehampton's Corporation could concentrate on important internal matters instead. Or so they thought. The Mayor and Burgesses:– had received a special writ

> *Nov. 1636, xxx" [£30] Collected for Ship money pd to the Sher[iffe] (Dennis Roole Esqr) of Devon.*

There was some indignation in the Corporation over this latest imposition but life in the town went on much the same as before in spite of the growing tide of unrest throughout the country.

> *May 8. 1639. The Pound within the Borough made up this summer, and the keeping thereof granted to William Weeks for his life, and after him to Johane, his daughter, for life they dwelling where he, the sayd William Weeks now dwelleth, and repayring the same, after it's new made, & for it he and she are to have the pound fees, vz, of the inhabitants of the borough 1d. and of strangers 4d. by agrement between Mr. Mayor and others and the said William Weeks, under their hands in the Towne booke the 18th of April 1639. This pound was made up with posts and railes many years since.*

News arrived that people were taking up arms against the imposition of the English Prayer Book once again – this time in Scotland.

> *1639, This year many companyes of soldyers, which came out of Cornwall, prest for the north against the Scotts, with the captaynes and officers travelling this way were lodged here, and passed quyetly. Special care being taken for billetting of them, and a vigilant watch set during night.*

The burgesses were taking no chances this time!

> *[1640] This year a writt procured by the Rt. Honble Jno Ld. Mohun, Baron Mohun of Okehampton, was brought to Mr Mayr: and the Burgesses & inhabitants here for the choice of Burgesses for the Parliament, wch privledge this Borough had in ancient tymes as by the record in the Tower of London appeareth.*

At last there was a chance to have the borough's voice heard in Parliament and to have a say in the bigger issues of the day. King Charles had been forced to recall Parliament in order to get support to suppress the rebellion north of the border. The election did not go without controversy locally however:–

> *January [1641]. At the eleccon [election] day after the publishing of Mr. Sheriffe of Devon, his warrt. on the sd. writt 4 or 5 days before, two Gent. vz., Laurence Whittaker, Esq: and Edward Thomas Esq: recomended by*

the sd. Lord Mohun before, the sd. Mr. Thomas was chosen by genall consent in the 1 place, the said Mr. Whittaker named, and with him Sr. Shilstone Calmady Kt, (not before heard of, by the Mayor and Burgesses here) Mr. Whitaker had the most voices [votes], And he and Mr. Thomas certified by Indenture between the Sherriff and the towne Whereupon Sr. Shilstone Calmady came hither shortly after & endeavoured a newe eleccon & required Mr. Mayor to have the Town Seal to seal another indenture which Mr. Mayor and the Burgesses denied him, whereupon Sr. Shilstone delivered some peticon [petition] to Parliament, wch tooke no effect.

1641, The Protestation sent from parliament now taken by Mr. Mayor and the burgesses and assistants present and by divers others and also by all or the most part of the town and parish of Okehampton.

By the Protestation return Okehampton and the rest of Devon declared in favour of the true, reformed, Protestant religion. There were many in the town whose extreme puritan views lead them to forthrightly condemn customs and practices that had been enjoyed for countless generations. The colour, youthful vigour and undertones of the ancient fertility rituals demonstrated at the onset of spring in particular were too much for some.

This year was some disorder committed in setting up a may-pole here, and some stirr touching it afterwards at the town sessions.

But there were other, potentially more serious rumblings on the horizon and it became increasingly difficult to conduct everyday business in the town.

17 Jan: 1641. An order made by genall consent that the room under the Court house shod be fitted, and employed for a roome to sell corn & wheat in, for some moderate toll; and it was desired & appointed that Mr. Bremelcombe Mr. Heaynes Mr. Parker Mr. Thomas Bidwell & Mr. Edmond Arscott undertake the same ...neglected by reason of the succeeding many troubles.

1642, The King's armyes and the parliaments armies came severally to this town, dyvers times this year, and quartered here, to the great dammage of the inhabitants. Mr. Mayor suffered very much both in his person and estate by some of the armies.

When the Civil War finally broke out, like most towns in the West of England, the Corporation was anxious not to take sides. Only Plymouth came down firmly on the side of Parliament. Most remained neutral in the hope that 'the troubles' would not touch too greatly upon them. Nevertheless, many men did cease their labours to take up arms on one side or the other – sometimes brother against brother or father against son. The tin works in the vicinity lay idle, mill wheels ceased turning and hungry mouths awaited their fathers' returns. These were desperate times once again.

May, 1643. The Fortification in stoney Parke was made by the direccon of Major James Chudleigh of the Parliament. army & there was a fight at Meldon downe by night in a great tempest of thunder and rain.

The earthworks were thrown up in a field adjoining the churchyard to guard the western approach to the town but the first clash between the opposing armies in the vicinity took place some four miles (6.5km) to the west and under the cover of darkness. The Royalist Army had withdrawn over the Tamar and a truce was agreed in the hope that the differences would be settled elsewhere. Young Major Chudleigh had other ideas though. Keen to see some action and make a name for himself, Chudleigh attacked the Royalists, under the command of Sir Ralph Hopton, at Launceston and, having repelled them, Hopton pursued them back over the Tamar but confusion reigned on both sides. The Sheriff of Cornwall was killed, men from both sides deserted at their first taste of hostilities and troops, guns and provision wagons were despatched in different directions! Hopkins, wishing to give Chudleigh a bloody nose for his impudence decided to make a surprise night attack on his remaining troops, numbering just over a hundred. To make certain that this irritation was wiped-out or driven off altogether he mustered 500 cavalry and 3,000 infantry troops and four cannon. In spite of this huge numerical advantage, most of his men lacked experience. Chudleigh, on the other hand, had luck on his side. By chance his quartermaster, looking for accommodation at Bridestowe, came upon the Royalists billeted there and brought warning.

As a result, Chudleigh was able to lay an ambush on the approaches to the town. Hopton's troops, feeling safe in their numbers approached the town with caution thrown to the wind while their officers were 'carelessly entertaining themselves'. When the cry was raised to attack, the Royalists were in complete disarray and half the Cornish army turned tail and ran with Chudleigh and a few of his men in hot pursuit. Only the cannon held their ground while the rest of the 'Roundheads' busied themselves emptying the pockets and packs of the fallen Royalist officers. Meanwhile Hopton fell back to Sourton Down and, fortuitously, found an old earthwork (*39*) and took up position with his musketeers in the trench and his other troops behind lines of pointed stakes. Two salvos from their cannon were enough to convince most of Chudleigh's remaining troops that they had pushed their luck far enough and panic set in. As Chudleigh doggedly charged again, lighting patches of gorse as decoys and then retreated, providence once again came to his aid and a violent storm suddenly erupted with thunder, lightning and hail stones putting the fear of God up the Royalist soldiers. Having spent a miserable night in the open, another storm the following morning sent them fleeing to Bridestowe.

Chudleigh's men came back to Okehampton in high spirits, claiming up to 120 dead and 500 wounded to their three or four wounded. The Parliamentarians had been doing rather badly up to that point and made maximum capital out of this small victory but the Royalists were soon to fight back and, after their victory at the battle of Stratton, they commanded most of Devon and Cornwall. The demands on the town continued.

June, 1643. A weekly paie begun towards the support of the army for the King, rated at 1 pound od money for this town and parish in Lifton hundred.

The weekly pay to the army contynued, and other taxes and payments with free quarter which was very chargeable to the inhabitants here this year. And Mr. Mayor and the constables very much troubled.

July 1, 1644, Queen Mary (Henrietta Maria) came hither with a great many and stayed 2 nights. Mr. Mayor gave to the Queen's servants of her guard £3—which was required of him.

The Queen was with her new-born baby, Henrietta, and preparing to flee to France. Although the centre of much attention, she received little sympathy as a reviled Catholic who many blamed for the King's troubles and the subsequent war.

July 2nd to the 19th, Prince Maurice with the King's army quartered here almost 3 weeks, during which tyme very many sheepe were plundered and killed, and eat by the soldiers, and the yeast hay and other provision of the inhabitants were spent.

One soldier was then hanged here in the street for plundering a house in Inwardley.

July 22, The Earle of Essex came with the L. Roberts, and the Parliament Army to a very great number, and very many carriages, but tarried but one night.

Came in Sir Robert Pye, Knight, with dyvers others to quarter, and towards night some skirmish was in the parish, and some killed which caused him and his company to depart suddenly that night.

King Charles came with many Lords and his army and staied one night. Mr. Mayor gave to his Maty's servants twenty pounds… being required by them with much earnestness. And to the Earl of Linsey his servants £3 11s. 0d.

John Rattenbury had the honour of providing hospitality to his Majesty in his house on this occasion and, naturally, treated him with due respect. However, he was understandably curious to see if he lived up to his reputation. He was left with the impression of an immensely dignified man, in spite of his small stature and slight stammer. He had little to say to his host however, merely giving a passing acknowledgement and yet he seemed to genuinely care about his subjects. He wore all the troubles of his realm on his brow now though and he took his leave, along with his entourage, with little ceremony. His wife and daughter might be in danger and he could not afford to lose the West to Parliament so he was taking an active part in the fighting and set off in hot pursuit of the Earl of Essex. These were desperate times indeed.

1644, Sir Richard Grenville, knight and baronet, quartered in this town several times, and divers other commanders, officers and souldiers.

This year the town was put to great costs for free quarter post-horses and convoy of letters by parliamentary souldiers and other such like as by Mr. Heayne's accompt may appear.

1645, This year in Oct. and Nov. Sir Richard Grenville did raise barricadoes and other works and made this town a garrison town for a while—free quarter continued till February.

Sir Thomas Fairfax, Generall of the Parliamt Army was here 2 days and marcht thence upon Easter-day 1646.

Within the space of a few short months Fairfax's 'New Model Army' had at last turned the war in Parliament's favour and mopped up the remaining resistance in the far corners of the south west of England. After the King was tried and executed, the country got used to life without a monarchy. John wondered what all the sacrifice was for. Things didn't seem any better for ordinary people somehow.

His journal entries returned to recording the mundane events and disputes of a small town as if the momentous upheavals of the previous five years had never happened. The sundry misdemeanours of the populace continued to meet with his disapproval and his patience and optimism seemed to decline with age. Relations between church and corporation hadn't improved much either. After all his years of unstinting service to the town, he was understandably mortified to be accused, along with other principal burgesses, of 'miscarriages' regarding the stewardship of endowments given for the benefit of the poor of the town.

> *6 Octo. 1651. There was a suit in Chauncery commenced by Wm. Turpin the two Churchwardens & the Overseers of the poore of Okehampton against the sayd Mr William Drew, Mr John Bremelcombe, Mr John Rattenbury, Mr John Shebbeare & Mr Christopher Drewe it was shortly after putt in Reference unto Mr Richard Mervin Clarke, Mr Thomas Finney Clarke & fower others gent. the suit was Commenced upon some pretences of miscarriages touching the towne & poore &c Suit stayed, the Arbitrators did make an award, And in the same award Ended, concluded in these words, Whereas wee doe finde Mr John Rattenbury to be much suspected & Questioned by the plaintiffs & others Concerning some miscarriages in the premises, Wee doe therefore think it Fitt to certify all whome it may concerne, That it doth appear to Us, he hath beene on[e] of the best Instruments to procure & preserve many (if not most) of the indowments belonging to the poore of this towne & parish of Okehampton, And att present one of the greatest helpes or the discovery of most of the particulers relating to this present arbitration. This wee doe affixe to our present award Under our Hands, Richard Marvin Thomas Finney &c.*

He was naturally at pains to ensure that this steadfast vindication was recorded for posterity lest the taint of suspicion should linger after his death, for he had always endeavoured to be an honourable gentleman. Not that the recipients of poor relief were always that honest themselves.

> *Oct 23, 1653. Mr Christopher Drewe, Mayor, upon Viewe & searching what Condition such poore people were in as had weekly pay & gathered alms daily here. Found in the Coffer of Joane Kelly Widow (being on[e] of that Number) Therty poundes twelve shillinges & nine pence, whose two former husbands, John Kelly & Wm. Blackford, had for a Long time weekly pay as in & by the Overseers accompts doth & may appear.*

Infirmity and old age were slowing John down but he remained in office until the last and was made one final gesture to make sure that posterity remembered him:–

> *Oct. 3, 1654. Mr. John Rattenbury, town clerk, presented to Mr. Mayor a little*

silver seale, having Okehampton town arms ingraven thereon, tyed with a black ribbon (as his legacy) to remain with him and his successors yearly while it lasteth.

Shortly afterwards his successor recorded:–

Mr. John Rattenbury, one of the principall burgesses dyed in this year 1655, having been Town Clerk & steward of the Borough Cort. for above 30 years, & in his time 4 times mayor of Okehampton, a great preserver of the records & priviledges belonging to this Towne and Borough. Richard Shebbeare.

THE COMMONWEALTH AND BEYOND

On Rattenbury's death, one Thomas Welles became Town Clerk but was removed from office for neglect of duties within just two short years. Thomas Austyn, who, following in the footsteps of Rattenbury, also kept a personal record of town affairs, succeeded him. Both journals were later faithfully copied and continued up to 1698 by Richard Shebbeare, thus providing a unique record of life in Okehampton through much of the seventeenth century.

The Commonwealth period in Okehampton gave the strongly puritan element among the town's justices the opportunity to impose their codes of morality with increased zeal. Not everyone was prepared to bow to their authority however. One Richard Bower refused to become a constable and was fined the large sum of £10, Peter Can, in a drunken rage, climbed onto the market cross waving his halberd like a madman. He was fined five shillings after being talked down by his wife. The burgesses were determined that this sort of behavior didn't rub-off on the 'younger sort'. When Thomas Fyner was appointed as Master of the Grammar School in 1652 he was ordered to ensure that the 'scholars behave themselves civilly and orderly in coming and going to and from school, and at the church and chapel'. These were also the days of witch-hunts and in 1658 four women were accused of witchcraft in the town. The evidence was extremely flimsy however. One complainant stated that "after the said Margery had been there" she could "never milk the said cows nor come where they were, but the said cows would run at her and bellow and endeavor to kill her"!

Ancient customs were banned. A fight started after a group of shoemakers' apprentices attempted to keep up their old custom of taking a horse head round on their August festival. They were assaulted by a pikestaff and ended up before the magistrates. Such customs, with their pagan undertones, were common in the early Stuart period. The parading of a horse's skull or snapping model head to raise money for the church guilds or simply for fun and ale, have parallels in the *Mari Lwyd* Christmastide rituals of south Wales and the spring *Hobby 'Oss* festivities of Padstow and Minehead. Morris dancing, plays or sports often accompanied such festivities. The authorities frowned upon all such activities during the Commonwealth period however. Even more genteel pastimes were banned. The bowling green (where the Drill Hall now stands in Mill Road) went out of use and a fulling rack (on which fulled cloth was stretched out to dry) was set up on it by Joseph Sprague. Everyone had to attend church on pain of heavy fines and strenuous efforts were made to ensure that the elderly and infirm weren't excluded – indeed a special handbarrow was employed for the purpose! Although the office of Bishop was removed, parish priests remained, in spite of an attempt to introduce a Presbyterian Church system in Devon. Civil registration of births and deaths were introduced though and marriage banns were called from the market cross and a justice of the peace rather than the vicar conducted the marriage services itself. Such changes were not universally welcomed and within a few years the vicar of Okehampton, Mr. John Hussey, was openly conducting marriage services in church again. This defiance appears to reflect the popular mood of the time and there was much rejoicing when the monarchy was restored with the return of Charles II. Soon after, Lewes Parker, a Puritan of extreme and outspoken views, was removed from the corporation, Puritan religious meetings were banned and a number of parishioners were excommunicated. The pendulum of popular support had now swung against their followers and, in 1676, Mr. Hussey recorded only one Papist and seven dissenters amongst his 1,207 parishioners. Many lessons had been learned during the religious upheavals of the preceding century and a half and a more tolerant society was eventually to emerge.

In spite of the return of a monarchy, the principle of parliamentary government was now firmly established. It was still far from democratic in the modern sense however. Only freemen and freeholders – representing less than twn per cent of the total population of Okehampton parish – had a vote and their support was often bought. For instance, in the election of 1676, Squire Henry Norleigh was elected to represent the borough with 102 *voyces* or votes over his rival, Josias Calmady of Leawood, Bridestowe with 48. To achieve this result, Norleigh spent no less than £460 entertaining voters at six inns in the town – working out at almost £5 a vote – a considerable sum for the time. It represented more than a year's wages for most. A system of organized poor relief by the parish had been introduced with the Poor Law of 1601. This was not universally popular with those well enough off to be required to pay the poor rates that supported it however. Nevertheless, many of the better off in society did take their social responsibilities seriously and charitable giving and bequests were relatively high in seventeenth century Okehampton. The victims of a fire in the same year received a gift of £5 from the Duke of Albermarle and £10 from the 'county stocke' for their relief. Almost a century before, in 1588, Richard Brock left a house and meadow in Castle Lane to provide accommodation and allotments for two elderly inhabitants and £60, the annual profit from which was to be lent to poor tradesmen. In 1638, his daughter, Grace Brock, willed that £10 should be given towards the upkeep of these almshouses on her death. In 1623, Richard Harragroe left £2 for the repair of the church and a like sum for the organ, £40 *'towards a stock for employing the industrious poor of the town and parish'* (except Kigbeare hamlet). Harragroe clearly recognized the benefits of education for those same poor, however. For it was he who left £50 to provide the £5 a year supplement to the annual salary of the Grammar School master so that the six or eight poor children nominated by the Mayor *"may be brought up in the fear of God and good letters for ever"*. It wasn't always a case of 'charity begins at home' either. Money was frequently collected for the relief of victims of plague and fires elsewhere in the County and even further afield. Okehampton people reached into their coffers on hearing of the Great Plague of London, for instance, and sent £6 9s 5¼d to assist the families of victims. In 1670 Shebbeare recorded *'Collected by Mr. John Hussey, and Cosin Benjamin Gayer for and towards the relief of poor protestants taken in Turkey, the charity of the inhabitants of this town and parish, and there was gathered ten pounds and odd money.'* Thereby hangs a tale.

It is said that 'Cosin Benjamin' was as interested in releasing his captured cargoes as the seamen ransomed by the Turkish pirates. He died in 1700 and, for his 'sins', he is said to have been condemned to empty Cranmere Pool with a sieve and that his soul could not rest until the penance was complete. However, 'Cranmere Benjie', as he has become known, was too ingenious and lined the sieve with a sheepskin, thus flooding the town below. This and his wailing and bemoaning of his fate so disturbed the townsfolk that they had his spirit exorcised in the form of a black colt which was then ridden headlong into the pool by a young boy who jumped off at the last minute. Benjie was then given the fresh penance of weaving rope from grains of sand! In fact, Gayer was five times mayor of Okehampton and lived in a house near St. James Chapel, upon the gable of which his initials could be seen affixed. Until quite recently, these could still be seen on the back of Wright's Ironmongers, the building that replaced Gayer's house in 1895/6, and they are still enshrined in local folklore:–

> *"Behind the chantry mote be yred,*
> *The initial scroll of burgher dead;*
> *Stout of heart they esteem the wight*
> *Who reads those letters by dead of night.*
> *Though the moon be glinted back the while*
> *From the oriel lights of the chantry aisle;*
> *Never pass but breathe a prayer*
> *For the soul's best peace on Master Gayer"*

Mid 19th century view of St. James Chapel from the south east, prior to the re-building of the nave in 1862. The initials BG can be seen on the gable wall of Gayer's House to the left and the pillars of the guildhall can be seen through the gap. (Museum of Dartmoor Life)

Engraving after Rawlinson, published by M. Jones in 1806 of the old East Bridge, showing the market shambles, with steps leading up to the chamber over to the right. The tower of St. James can be seen in the centre but the tower in the distance is probably artistic licence as the parish church would not be visible from this angle. (Museum of Dartmoor Life)

Master Gayer may well have been a merchant with interests in far-off places but there is no evidence to suggest that he was anything other than an honest and well-meaning citizen.

As the century wore on, so the town prospered along with the rest of Devon, thanks, largely, to the flourishing wool trade. Four new mills were established and the market thrived. In 1666 Shebbeare records *'This year the wester Shambles were pulled down and new built, with a chamber over the Shambles, which was intended for a place to sell wheate in upon some small toolle, the said Chamber cost the corporacon a considerable sume'*. In 1676 two more fairs were granted including the ever popular March Fair. In 1682, John

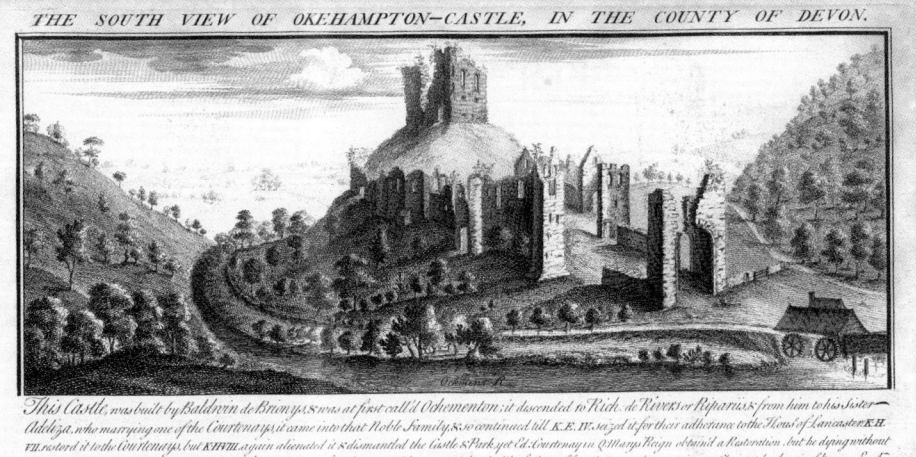

The ruins of Okehampton Castle as engraved by the brothers John and Nathaniel Buck in 1734 for their publication 'The Castles of England and Wales'. Note the double mill near the barbican gatehouse. (Museum of Dartmoor Life)

Ellacott, later Mayor of Okehampton, leased *'that gatehouse first entering into the old decayed castle of Okehampton'* and formed a dwelling, bakehouse and gardens within the ruined walls. The old water mill by the castle gate provided the flour and a discarded millstone can still be seen forming the base of one of his ovens in the old Western lodging of the castle. John Northmore, a freeman, attorney and Town Clerk, although relatively new to the town, leased Rattenbury's old house and built what is now the town hall as a private dwelling on the site in 1685. Its elegant and well-proportioned ashlar granite facade must have made quite an impression on the inhabitants and represented a statement of wealth that few could make in the vicinity. It was also symbolic of the dawning of a new age where the outside influences of fashion, art and architecture were to be introduced to the district by a growing 'middle class'.

In 1684, the town received a new Charter, but at a considerable cost. King Charles, faced with strong opposition from his parliament, forced parliamentary boroughs to surrender their old charters in a bid to control them by the power to remove any member of a corporation. In return, the Okehampton Corporation managed to get the jurisdiction of the borough courts extended to the parish. On 4th September 1684 Shebbeare records, no doubt with much self-satisfaction, *'Mr. Richard Shebbeare, now sworne mayor of the town, borough and parish of Okehampton, by virtue of the new charter, which was this very day brought home, accompanied by Sir George Cary, Knight, our Recorder, Sir Amos Pollard, Justice Gidley, Squire Burgoine, with divers gentlemen, magistrates and townsmen to the number of nigh two hundred horse and four drummers, two trumpeters, three weight players, bells ringing, with the trained bands, footemen and boys, &c.'*

After the brief reign of James II and the prospect of a return to Roman Catholicism as the main religion, Shebbeare records: *'19 Feb., 1688. This day William and Mary, prince and princesse of Orange were proclaymed kinge and queen of England, France and Ireland, and effigies of the Pope burnt in this towne.'* No doubt the ale flowed freely as the majority of townsfolk celebrated.

Perhaps Edward Reddaway celebrated a little too well for he was drowned in a pool beyond Beare Bridge *(40)* on his way home. There was further cause for celebration eight years later when a temporary peace with the old enemy from across the channel was announced: *26 Oct. 1697, This day the Lord's Justices' proclamacon was proclaimed at the Town hall, at the Crosse and at the Markett house Stairs..... wherein was signified that the King had concluded a peace with the French King, and a bonfire made down at Beare bridge.*

Meanwhile, there was an increase in the followers of non-conformist religions including Quakers and Presbyterians although in the early years they had no regular meeting houses.

Okehampton in the early eighteenth century might have been a more tolerant place in terms of religious beliefs, but wealth, class and station were still clearly defined. This was nowhere more clearly demonstrated than in church where the size and position of seats indicated the relative importance of their occupants who were *'seated according to their estate and quality'*. Inevitably this arrangement led to frequent disputes! The responsibilities placed on the parish by the Poor Law also gave rise to disputes over who was entitled to relief and who was responsible for giving it. Under the Laws of Settlement of 1662, welfare relief became the responsibility of the claimant's parish of origin. Casual labourers from other parishes had to provide a certificate from their home parish guaranteeing that they would take him back when his employment ended. Anyone from another parish trying to settle without any prospect of work within forty days could be removed unless they rented property to the value of £10 per annum. Vagabonds were definitely not welcome. Six were recorded between 1676 and 1685 – one man and five women, three of whom had young children – all were whipped and sent packing. As the poor rate rose, so the hundred or so ratepayers questioned the deservedness of the recipients. Even soldiers injured during the Civil War were accused of malingering, especially if they fought on the 'wrong side'. Pauper children were bound-out as apprentices in a variety of crafts or as farmhands and domestic servants by indenture. Support to the thirty or so regular recipients of poor relief, including the sick and the elderly, was usually in the form of food, shoes, clothes, fire wood or rent. Then there were the all too frequent shrouds for pauper burials. In addition to parish relief, various local charities continued to provide substantial support to the poor, elderly and infirm of Okehampton throughout the following two centuries before insurance schemes and, eventually, the 'welfare state' took over in the twentieth century.

The fortunes of the local wool trade fluctuated and declined through the eighteenth century as a series of European wars interrupted exports. Fashions changed also, away from the course serges produced in the vicinity until, eventually, the cheaper mass-production of the new industrial mills in the midlands and north forced many local merchants out of business. The prosperity of the town as a whole declined along with the wool trade as the eighteenth century progressed and it wasn't just the distant industrial areas that provided the competition. The town presented a petition to Parliament in 1796 complaining of the "decay of our Markets by reason of Spinning-houses being set up in the neighbourhood" and they made an unsuccessful attempt to stop neighbouring North Tawton from being granted a market. Even trade along the great highway through the town was threatened by the proposal to build a new road across Dartmoor to link Moretonhampstead with Tavistock. The town petitioned against this also without success. Waywardens collected money and looked after roads within the parish but the state of the roads generally was still very poor. By the middle of the century, the new turnpike trusts were making improvements to the long distance routes up country with money raised by tolls. In 1652, a journey from London would have taken about five days on horseback, travelling at an average speed of around three miles per hour. By

1764, passenger coaches were available between London and Exeter and the journey time was reduced to just over two days. Twenty years later and this had been reduced again to thirty two hours at an average speed of ten miles per hour. Transport by wheeled vehicle remained uncommon however, and most goods were still being moved around by packhorse or *truckamuck* (sled). Indeed, this was the situation until well into the nineteenth century in the most remote parts of the district. As a result, few people travelled very far from home and, for most, a horse was still a luxury. Marriage and work were the main reasons for leaving one's native parish and, even then, the distances weren't great.

Younger sons of farming families also tended to move 'abroad' to seek a farm of their own. Apart from the land-holding yeoman farmers, many farms and small holdings were held on a 'three-life lease' whereby the leaseholder paid a heavy 'fine' upon taking it up and, thereafter, a modest reserved rent. The arrangement continued until three named lives – potentially three generations – had succeeded or 99 years had elapsed, but the lease could be extended on the payment of a further fine and, in this way, a farm could be held by the same family for centuries. Although there was no one major land owner or 'squire' in Okehampton until the 1800s, land and property ownership was still the privilege of a small minority and, increasingly, parliamentary representation tended to be from outsiders who were mainly interested in the parliamentary privileges ownership of property in the borough bestowed. During the eighteenth and nineteenth centuries, for instance, MPs for the borough included members of the Pitt and Spencer families – the latter were ancestors of Diana, Princess of Wales. Among the more famous representatives were Clive of India and William Pitt the Elder, later the Earl of Chatham. Pitt was elected MP for Okehampton in 1756 – the same year that he commenced his first term as Prime Minister. The Pitts were not entirely uninterested in the borough which gave them their seats however, Thomas Pitt presented a fire engine, which was kept in the tower of St. James's chapel, but, as with most 'rotten boroughs', bribery and corruption were commonplace until the town eventually lost its parliamentary franchise in 1832.

In spite of increasing outside influences, life in the town changed slowly. It was far-removed from the fashionable Regency spa towns of Bath and Cheltenham – both geographically and socially – although John Hockin, vicar from 1744 to 1778, thought a physician might 'analize and recommend' the local mineral springs to that effect. 'High society' probably consisted of private dinner parties, taking tea and playing cards or the occasional concert or ball at one of the 'great houses' of the district. Conversation on the issues of the day might have been instigated by the few who received the Exeter Flying Post newspaper. More commonly though, it probably revolved around the activities of the 'lower orders' in the vicinity and any local scandal, for many of the population were still unruly in spite of the ongoing efforts of the church and corporation! Occasionally there would have been visitors or travellers staying at one of the town inns to gossip about. Although Dartmoor didn't quite offer the dramatic alpine or gentle pastoral scenery favored by the artists of the day, its beauty and rugged grandeur were recognized, along with the picturesque rural charm of its inhabitants and their rustic dwellings. J. M. Turner among others came and drew inspiration from the castle's romantic, ivy-clad ruins for

Engraving of the ivy-clad ruins of Okehampton Castle by S. Middiman from a drawing by J. C. Smith. (Museum of Dartmoor Life)

instance, employing his characteristic artistic license on the scene. The Buck brothers produced a more faithful reproduction for their great volume 'The Castles of England & Wales' (published in 1734) and another famous view by Richard Wilson (1714-82) following his visit in 1771, was probably the one he exhibited at the Royal Academy in 1774 and which now hangs in Birmingham City Museum and Art Gallery.

The castle also attracted the attentions of a young French naval officer, Gilles A. Vincent, while he was held on parole in the borough in 1809 following his capture at sea on 10th June of that year. During his visit he carved the words "HIC V .....T FUIT CAPTIVUS BELLI" (Here Vincent was a prisoner of war) into the side of the piscina in the chapel, thus leaving his mark to this day. Vincent was a surgeon on the French Man o' War named "Rejoirie" and obviously well-educated. Unlike many of his compatriots, he and his fellow officers enjoyed relatively comfortable accommodation, were given the freedom to roam within a mile radius of their parole town and a modest allowance, provided they obeyed certain rules and attended a twice weekly roll-call. The lower ranks, by contrast, had to endure the squalid conditions of the prison 'hulks' (disused ships) in Plymouth Sound or within the crowded walls of the newly built prison at Princetown where many died from diseases caused by such close confinement and unsanitary conditions.

Between 1809 and 1812, 336 prisoners were quartered in the town when the population stood at around 1,500. They were mainly French naval officers (162) although there were 131 army officers, personal servants, civilian merchants and even wives and children among them. They were surprisingly well-received by the townsfolk. Perhaps this was because of the spending power provided by their allowances or the funds sent by their families, which they were allowed to draw through local banks. Maybe some were valued as a source of cheap labour or for their particular skills – teaching languages for instance – or could it have simply been their romantic allure! Local tradition holds that French POW's were responsible for laying the cobbles of the Choir Boys' Path leading towards the church and were involved in various building works. The old warehouse off West Street, in which the Museum of Dartmoor Life is now housed, bears the date of 1811 on the keystone of the door arch and is of an unusual form of architecture for the district – could this be an example of their handiwork? Others supplemented their allowances by teaching music, drawing or sword skills to the local gentry. Some prisoners are said to have been billeted in an old barn in Fairplace while others lodged with local families or rented rooms or houses in the town. Most of the wives and children were repatriated and there were, no doubt, more than a few romantic liaisons with local girls, indeed five marriages are recorded in the parish registers. Sadly some were never to return to their native soil for other reasons though. At least four, including a women who died in childbirth, are buried in the churchyard. Some inevitably escaped – twenty seven on one occasion, only three of whom were re-captured. Those not so well-off were perhaps driven to taking food unlawfully. Pierre Millet, for example, was charged with steeling leeks and onions from the garden of Thomas Gliddon, a tailor.

The threat of invasion in 1812 led the authorities to move the prisoners to Scotland and the north of England for fear of insurrection in such an event. Local volunteers forces were also mustered to counter such threats. The Loyal Okehampton Infantry Regiment was formed in 1806 with a strength of 200 officers and men, resplendent in their uniforms of "blue pantaloons and scarlet jackets faced with yellow". Following Napoleon's final defeat at Waterloo in 1815, Okehampton once again played host to French prisoners of war – this time sixty six battle-weary veterans who were returned to France as soon as peace was concluded, thus ending what must have been an exciting and colourful episode in the town's history.

WHEN SQUIRE RULED ALL

Albany Savile sat by the window of his study, clutching a balance sheet and staring across the ornamental lake to the tightly packed roofs of the town, nestling beneath East Hill beyond. A glass of port stood on the table beside him and his foot rested on a gout stool. Albany was a stout man with a ruddy complexion that gave away his love of high living. His country seat was Oaklands Mansion, on the edge of Okehampton, and he also had a town house in Park Street, Westminster. He was forty-seven years of age and married to Eleanora, daughter of Sir Bourchier Wrey, squire of Tawstock near Barnstaple. She had born him no less than eight sons and five daughters in the previous fourteen years. He was an only son and had two sisters, Cordelia and Henrietta. In 1830, Squire Savile would hardly have needed any introduction in the district. He was every inch the archetypal country squire and he had made it his business to dominate local politics, business and community life. Although outwardly self-confident to the point of overbearing, he was basically a rather insecure man. His over-riding mission in life was to obtain respectability in any way he could. The respect he so desired was largely given unquestionably by his servants and tenants but his peers and the freemen of Okehampton were another matter. He was ever conscious that his status was not conferred by birth.

Savile's father, a Yorkshireman named Christopher Savile, was actually born Christopher Atkinson and was a common merchant, albeit a highly successful one. By the time of his death in 1819 he had amassed a sizeable fortune. In 1798 he had married Jane Savile, the daughter of a gentleman named John Savile of Enfield in Middlesex and immediately adopted her surname in order to acquire greater respectability. However, this was not to come easily nor without cost. He was a contractor for the army and navy and in 1785 had suffered the indignity of having to stand in a pillory in front of a large crowd of onlookers outside of the Corn Exchange in Mark Lane, London, having been accused of shady dealing in connection with the purchase of malt from the Navy Victualling Board. His humiliation was very public and became the talk of society. The Gentleman's Magazine had recorded how he '*stood for one hour, according to his sentance, for perjury. He was dressed in a light coloured coat, his hair dressed and powdered, and he bowed to the populace three times before he went in. A great concourse of people were assembled, and the Sherrifs attended on horseback, with their officers, the two City Marshalls, and upwards of 500 Constables. Labels were stuck upon the pillars of the Corn Market, "Christopher Atkinson Esq For Perjury."*' Since his death, Albany had been determined to erase this slur against the family name and to use his inherited wealth and self-made position to gain the political power necessary to re-write the family's history and 'win friends and influence' in his own right.

The small 'pocket borough' of Okehampton was ideally suited to Albany's aspirations. His late father had had the foresight to acquire the patronage of the borough by purchasing numerous freeholds and thereby controlling its two precious parliamentary seats (he already had one in his control back in his native Yorkshire). Albany wasted no time in getting himself elected to one of them – first in 1807 then 1812 and 1818 – on the last occasion sharing the honours with his father just a year before his death. The 'privilege' cost him a considerable sum however, votes didn't come cheap, even though there weren't that many entitled to vote in the first place. What money didn't buy he achieved by influence or intimidation. By marrying Eleanora in 1815 he effectively bought his way into the local 'squirearchy' and began to acquire the land and influence to go with the rank. For instance, he was Recorder for the borough and as such, administered the oaths of office to members of the corporation as well as presiding over the quarter sessions. Although the recorder was elected each year by the mayor and burgesses, this was something of a formality as Savile either nominated or insisted on approving all candidates for municipal office or membership of the corporation in the first place. In fact, he paid a generous stipend to many of them so, naturally, he could depend on their loyalty. As recorder and patron of the borough he was also instrumental in establishing a system whereby the office of mayor was inextricably linked with that of Justice of the Peace. He was also a Trustee of the Okehampton Turnpike Trust and had interests in various boards and commercial ventures. In other words, he had the borough, his tenants, trade, industry and local justice all firmly within his control.

He even had virtual supremacy over spiritual matters as both a Churchwarden and patron of the living. This he had granted to his brother-in-law in 1822. Savile's eldest son, Albany Bourchier, was a promising heir to his estates and title of squire. As was common practice among the gentry, his second son, Bourchier Wrey, was being prepared for a comfortable living with the Church under his father's patronage. He was a scholar at Westminster School and destined to study theology at Cambridge. Albany could thus rest assured that Saviles would to rule mind, body and soul in the district for many years to come. The only cloud on the horizon was his growing debts. He found it hard to accept that he had squandered the immense fortune of nigh on half a million pounds that he had inherited just eleven short years before. He trusted that posterity would see his extravagance as a wise investment though when young Albany reaped the rewards. After all, power and influence could only be supported by an outward show of wealth and rank.

Savile had leased Northmore's elegant but fairly modest town house from the corporation while his mansion was built but preferred to reside most of the time at Mount Radford House, a large mansion in St. Leonards, Exeter. Mount Radford belonged to his friend, Sir Thomas Baring of the famous banking family. The Northmore House lease was terminated in 1825 so that the Corporation could convert it into a more suitable town hall in place of the small and dilapidated Guildhall in Middle Row. Albany's new home was chosen well. The property was then aptly named Sweetlands for 'sweet' his hard-won lands were indeed. The old stone and slate house had served its purpose well when he had first moved to Okehampton but it was not grand enough for his designs. The new mansion was named 'Oaklands' in a subtle attempt to suggest a more ancient, almost feudal, link with 'Oakhampton' (as the name was more commonly spelt in those days). In much the same way that Okehampton's Norman castle had been built to symbolise dominance over the nearby population, so too was Oaklands, only this time it was the classical lines of a

Engraving of Oaklands Mansion by T. Allom and W. Taylor, published in 1831. The town can be seen to the left and the tower of the parish church in the centre distance. (Museum of Dartmoor Life)

Greek temple that provided the symbolism rather than the military stronghold of the Norman lords. His architect, Charles Vokins of Pimlico, had done a fine job in creating such a neo-classical masterpiece with its fine symmetry and the massive pink sandstone columns of the porticoes supporting pediments that successfully hid all of the chimneys. The walls were of rendered stone, lined internally with brick, which also formed all of the internal walls and partitions. The bricks were made just across the river, from local clay, and each and every one bore Albany Savile's initials.

From the newly constructed Lodge Road from the town centre *(41)* ran the main drive past the circular rustic lodge. To the left there was a steep, wooded slope which formed a dramatic natural backdrop to the mansion. There were informal lawns, grazed by sheep and deer, spreading down to the river on one side and an ornamental lake, formal lawns, flower beds and a walled kitchen garden on the other. Beyond the house were the stables and kitchen court. The interior of the mansion was lavishly appointed with handsome wainscoting and an ostentatious display of the latest furnishings to impress any guests. On the ground floor there were an entrance hall, library, drawing room, dining room, breakfast room, study and the great staircase. Albany's favourite room was the billiard room. Great care had been taken to ensure the levelling, stability and proper lighting of the billiard table itself. It was lighted by a lantern (skylight) above – the exact size of the table below – and a large stained-glass window. This could be viewed directly from the entrance hall 300 feet away. The flat roof of the billiard room formed a flower balcony to his wife's dressing room. The entrance hall itself was very impressive with its glass domed roof and array of niches – each bearing a classical statue. The whole house was centrally heated by a large boiler in the basement and there were ample, well appointed bedrooms for family and guests on the first floor, each with hot water, a dressing room and water-closet, as well as the well-used nurseries! The basement naturally contained well-stocked wine cellars and the service wing incorporated kitchens, pantries, bakehouses and brewhouses, and the servants' hall. In addition, there were all manner of service rooms on the ground and first floors – interconnected by a separate staircase of course.

The household and estate were kept up by an army of servants: butlers and housekeepers; governess and nannies; cooks; coachmen and footmen; grooms, gardeners and gamekeepers; farm workers and craftsmen and numerous chamber, parlour, kitchen and scullery maids. Many of them 'lived in' in the servants' quarters in the attic or above the stables and were grateful for the security of a roof over their heads and work in the 'big house'. Most considered it a privilege to serve the Squire. Indeed, it was true, there were far worse occupations and dwelling places in the district and it was a foolish individual who would choose the life of a pauper rather than give-over their lives and pledge obedience to a master. In fact, Savile was a kindly and generous man and any young apprentice bound to him would do well enough, provided they 'knew their place' and didn't steal from him. With all of the tasks of running the estate taken care of, Albany could concentrate on the leisurely pursuits appropriate to his station – fox hunting, shooting, fishing, breeding horses (and children), entertaining guests, carrying out ceremonial duties in the district and playing at politics. His hospitality and generosity were well-known in the locality. In 1821, on Christmas Eve, he had marked the completion of Oaklands by hosting a dinner, in a temporary room fitted-out for the occasion, for all of the hundred or so craftsmen and labourers employed on its construction. A band had accompanied the meal, which was washed down, enthusiastically, by large quantities of strong beer and spirits. Savile had invited members of the corporation and local gentry along to witness the occasion and his generosity, from a raised stage. Later, wives and sweethearts had been allowed to join the men for a dance and Albany remembered, with great satisfaction, their cheery voices as they departed, singing his praises as their new, most charitable, benefactor. He had made his mark on the little town sure enough!

But without investments and land and the income they provided he could not keep up these appearances for long. He had inherited the castle and manor on his father's death in 1819. He now owned thousands of acres in the vicinity, including much of the common land. In spite of his generous nature, as owner he considered himself master of all – including his servants and tenants - as of right. He was certainly no respecter of the ancient and customary rights of the little burgesses. They had once had the audacity to challenge his desire to purchase rights over 500 acres of common – his land — so he had 400 acres of it ploughed up just to spite them. In fact, he was a little unscrupulous when it came to land matters generally. He owed the Corporation close on £500 for the purchase of income from leaseholds but he knew they would not dare speak out against him so he was happy to leave it a while longer. After all, they had done well under his patronage and the town's appearance and economy had benefited greatly from his schemes and influence.

The Turnpike Trust for instance (formed after an Act of Parliament back in 1760) had recently completed several new stretches of road within the parish. For example, New Road to the west avoided the steep assent of Sharp or Shob Hill (High Street) and Lodge Road provided a more direct route to the north.

There were four tollhouses – one controlling each of the above, another in North Lane (North Street) and one at the entrance to the newly-built Barton Road. These not only provided income for maintenance and further improvements to the parish roads, pavements and bridges but also accommodation and employment. The market had been re-located to the area of Lodge Road and the old market shambles, Guildhall and parts of the dilapidated Middle Row were to be pulled down in due course, thus improving sanitation and reducing the risk of fire. Then there was the railway scheme that he was pursuing with his neighbours, Squire John Morth Woollcombe of Ashbury and Squire Calmady-Hamlyn of Bridestowe. They had engaged Mr. Roger Hopkins, an engineer, to survey the land between Okehampton and Bideford with a view to constructing a railway line linking the two towns. It would then be possible to transport goods and passengers behind one of those wonderful new inventions – the steam locomotive. An earlier plan to link up with the Bude Canal at Holsworthy had come to nothing due to the challenging terrain and lack of capital. Savile had heard of the success of Stevenson's Stockton to Darlington railway line through his connections in the north of England and was keen to be seen as a pioneer himself, as well as reaping the financial rewards such a venture might provide.

'Bus House', the old tollhouse on the Hatherleigh approach, from an unsigned watercolour of the late 19th century. (Okehampton Town Council)

Limestone was a particularly valuable commodity in these parts, as it was essential for improving the acid soils of the district. A number of small quarries already operated in the vicinity; at nearby Meldon for instance, but delays at the kiln mouth and the state of the country roads made the business slow and expensive. Carriers had to queue up to be loaded whilst the laborious process of burning the lime in the kiln was carried on. Hopkins considered that the increased quantities of cheaper material available from larger quarries further afield, and the accompanying reduction of transport costs, alone would justify the construction costs. Then there would be the indirect benefit of a reduction in the poor rates brought about by the employment of hundreds of labourers during its construction. The population had practically doubled in the past ten years and there were real hardships for many due to unemployment or under-employment. But it was the cost of their relief that worried Savile most – it was better that they worked for their living in his opinion. Transporting any goods by road over long distances was still fraught with difficulties too, in spite of the appearance of many new turnpike roads across the county. The network of rough and muddy packhorse tracks that still linked them was the main problem and the frequent extraction of tolls from the various turnpike trusts across the county was hardly an inducement to long-distance trade. Hopkins also talked of savings on the carriage of coal imports and the increased value of timber exports as well as the possibility of establishing factories in the district ultimately. This prospect worried Savile however, as an influx of labourers from other areas might introduce seeds of discontent that would upset the balance in his cosy little 'empire'.

As it was, the new trade unions springing up to the north had yet to find any real support in rural Devon and the only dissent against the order of things was channelled through the increasing number of non-conformist churches in the vicinity. The popular Wesley brothers had passed through the town several times over half a century before while preaching in Devon and Cornwall and these visits were still talked of in the locality. On one occasion, in 1744, John Wesley had preached to a crowd of Quakers, who then formed the larger part of the population of nearby Sticklepath, from a rock on The Mount above the village during a terrible hail storm and yet they had stood unflinching throughout. As Wesley had put it 'their souls took acquaintance'. There was something about the fervour of lay preachers that Albany found slightly unnerving. They had a passion and conviction about them unlike most of the neglectful and conservative clergy who enjoyed comfortable livings in the Anglican Church. This was especially so when it came to condemning ostentation and the injustices they claimed existed in society – but, being God-fearing men and women, thankfully they only fought with words. He had heard of riots elsewhere in the country and so he continued to keep a firm grip on the local justice system as a precaution. He was aware of especially strong opposition close to home from the recently formed Bible Christian movement that had been founded at nearby Shebbear by a Cornish farmer, William O'Bryan, back in 1815. O'Bryan had witnessed John Wesley preach as a boy and was presented to him in 1789. Wesley had reportedly placed his hands on his head saying, "May he be a blessing to hundreds and thousands". He was reputedly something of a 'hothead' then and was actually expelled from the Methodist Church for failing to obey their rules. O'Bryan himself was no longer a threat though, as he had split from the movement he had established and emigrated to America the year before. Nevertheless, his influence lived on in the district. From the small beginnings of 1815 when twenty two like-minded people had met together in a farmhouse, the church now had some 10,000 members and had become a popular focus for religious and secular discontent.

Sunday schools provided limited education to the masses but most received no formal education at all. The old grammar school had been defunct since 1806 but some children from better-off households attended private 'dame schools' where mistresses taught the rudimentary skills of reading and writing. Only the sons of the gentry had a real opportunity to obtain anything like a full education however, including attending university – and that was how it should have been in Albany's opinion. What would the labouring classes (or wives of gentlemen come to that) want with educating? It could only lead to trouble, giving them ideas above their station and leading to yet more discontent. Next they'd be wanting the vote! (he did not even conceive of the notion of women having such a right). Learning a trade or how to serve was another matter and something that had his whole-hearted support. The main trades in the vicinity were still spinning and weaving. There had been a modest recovery in the wool industry, in spite of increasing competition from elsewhere and the town and immediate district had over 500 looms in operation – the third highest number in the county in fact. This was still mainly a cottage industry though and there was little chance of any organised dissent from individual cloth workers scattered about the town and district so, for the time being, Albany could rest easy.

Aside from the wool trade, there were the traditional occupations of glove making, leather tanning, milling, thatching, slating and stone masonry. Most dwellings and outhouses were built of either cob or the very hard local metamorphic rock. Dressed granite, sandstone and brick were only employed in the buildings of the wealthiest inhabitants and the better-off farmers of the district. The stone was either quarried locally or worked from the plentiful surface 'moorstone' (granite). Apart from building stone and limestone, there were a small number of tin mines still working on the moor (*42*). There was increasing work for wainwrights (cart makers) and wheelwrights however, with the improving roads and the growing use of wheeled vehicles for transportation and travel in the vicinity, not to mention the influx of through traffic along the highway into Cornwall. The drivers of wagon trains and the fast passenger and mail carrying stage coaches stopped over at the burgeoning coaching inns while their horses were stabled overnight. Guests could enjoy refreshments and a welcome rest from their bumpy and dusty journeys. Albany had experienced the arduous journey to London himself on enough occasions, either on business or to attend society functions and, occasionally, to take up his seat in the House of Commons for some important debate or other. Though the journey time of less than two days was somewhat faster than it used to be and the coaches were now sprung, he wished that there was some easier and quicker way of making it. Maybe the railway had the potential to link little Okehampton with the great metropolis. What would the implications of that be? Would it help to repair his dwindling fortune? Would it bring civil unrest? Would the scaremongers be right about the dangers to health of travelling at speeds of upwards of twenty miles per hour or going through tunnels?

In between visits, Albany would keep up to date with affairs in the capital through newspapers and correspondence brought by the Royal Mail coaches. He would listen out eagerly by the study window for the sound of the horn that announced their approach from across the valley. He liked to think that the horn was a salute to him but really it was to warn the gate keeper to open the toll bar and let them through free of charge as the law decreed. The Turnpike Trust's finances were fairly healthy anyway so it was of no consequence. In between receiving news of the wider world there was plenty to amuse him closer to home with the goings-on of the inhabitants. It was not beneath his dignity to sit in the drawing room with the vicar or neighbouring squires and exchange the latest gossip and laugh heartily at the misfortunes of some poor fool or wretch. For instance, he had recently been told of a man from Lewtrenchard who 'bought' his wife from her husband at Okehampton market for half a crown and led her home some twelve miles with a halter round her neck! Apparently this was is something of a local custom and considered perfectly legal by the natives (*43*). Then there were the annual pleasure fairs where farmhands would come from miles around to enjoy a little fun and frivolity away from the day-to-day drudgery of their regular lives. What a spectacle they and the young maidens they pursued so amorously made! The first Saturday after Christmas was known as the Giglet Fair. A *giglet* was a 'giddy maid', the custom being that giglets could openly make their availability known and that young men could make free with them on such occasions. Custom dictated that "even the most rustic swain, if weary of his bachelorship" was "privileged with the right of self-introduction to any disengaged fair one who may take his particular fancy". There were stalls selling various sweetmeats and trinkets, plenty to eat and drink (usually paid for by their master if they were in work) and a fiddler who would lead a dance in an old barn later in the day. For those who were not in work or were seeking new employment for the coming season, it was also a hiring fair. Often the drink and excitement would get too much and brawls would break out or such passions aroused that young girls would do things that they would later bitterly regret. Albany was not so amused or understanding when their illegitimate offspring become a charge on the poor rate. There was a certain hypocrisy to such a perspective however as it was not uncommon for maid servants to find themselves in similar straits at the hands of their masters.

Over indulgence had taken its toll and Savile's health was declining so he decided not to stand for election to Parliament again that year. These were turbulent times politically and the Whigs (later to become the Liberals) were pushing hard for parliamentary reform. They claimed that it was not right that places like Okehampton, with a population of less than 3,000, should have two

Early 19th century engraving by G. Townsend of soldiers in New Road with the castle ruins beyond, published by H. Besley, Exeter. (Museum of Dartmoor Life)

representatives while large new industrial towns like Manchester and Birmingham had none. Industrialists and the new urban middle class were just trying to challenge the rightful power and influence of landowners in Savile's view and he failed to see how this would benefit his tenants and workers, let alone his own interests. Naturally, he had always been a staunch Tory and was a loyal supporter of the Duke of Wellington's government but an incident just prior to the election had made him act rather rashly. He had gone to London on business and planned to see Lord Chancellor Lyndhurst. However, Lyndhurst had declined to receive him and the snub so incensed Savile that he came home and put up two Whig candidates instead, just to spite him! Lord Seymour and Agar Ellis had duly been elected along with the first Whig government in fifty years but, alas, they too were in favour of reform and looked set to vote that way in the Commons when the opportunity arose.

Albany Savile's hopes of creating a dynasty founded on wealth, power, political influence and, above all, respectability for his successors, was looking somewhat forlorn. He had expended a huge proportion of the fortune he had inherited in pursuit of this ideal and now he appeared to have unintentionally sown the seeds of destruction for the political influence that supported it. On the other hand, he had much to be thankful for. He had a loving and doting family, some good friends and most of his staff and tenants treated him with genuine deference. Only history would declare whether this respect was earned or just bought along with everything else.

REFORM, EDUCATION AND IMPROVEMENT

Early in the year following the general election of 1830, Squire Albany Savile died, heavily in debt. Shortly after, in a twist of irony, Savile's candidates followed their consience and the Reform Bill was passed in the House of Commons by just one vote! It was finally accepted by the House of Lords in 1832 and, with it, local landowners lost the right to 'nominate' parliamentary candidates, the number of people entitled to vote doubled and Okehampton lost its parliamentary franchise and all the influence that went with it. The planned railway to Bideford was never built as insufficient capital was raised. In fact it would be another forty years before the railway finally reached the town. Young Albany Savile came of age in 1837 and sold Oaklands to Mr. James Hunt Holley of Norfolk in 1858. He then moved to Bristol and become a partner in a bank. He died, childless, in 1873. His younger brother, Rev. Bourchier Wrey Savile did indeed become Vicar of Okehampton between 1841 and 1847, thus maintaining the family link with the town. When his elder brother died, however, rather than leaving the remaining family estate to Bourchier, it was divided between all of Albany senior's numerous children, thereby bringing the dynasty to a very modest conclusion. The total dominance of the town by the local squire died with old Albany. Others were to attempt to exert similar influence much later but the seeds of true democracy had already been sown.

For most inhabitants, especially the least well off, life changed slowly however. The parish overseers of the Poor Law found it increasingly difficult to raise sufficient money from rates to provide relief for the ever-growing number of people in need, swelled all the more by labourers working on the roads and their dependants. Ignorance and the lack of birth control, combined with malnutrition, poor housing and a lack of proper sanitation caused overcrowding, high infant mortality, disease and severe hardship for many. Society frowned upon illegitimacy and single parenthood and families were expected to look after sick, disabled or elderly relatives when, in effect, many could barely look after themselves. Ignorance or indifference among the better off meant that many of these problems were considered self-inflicted and resulting from licentious behaviour or low morals generally. Some resented having to pay to support their fellows through the poor rate although charitable giving continued. Fortunately, some did recognise the value of education, full employment and opportunity, however. Charity schools carried on the work of the defunct grammar school in providing a rudimentary education until the

National School (at the southern end of North Street) was formed in 1837, while private 'dame' schools continued to teach the children of better off families, including many of the local tradesmen. It wasn't until the Board School, further along North Street, was built in 1877 that compulsory elementary education for both boys and girls was introduced. However, 'mitching' (truancy) was common. There were just too many temptations on the doorstep – 'scrumping' for apples in someone's orchard or searching for birds' eggs, not to mention games of hide and seek! Children also often played truant to help with the harvest. By the end of the century, non-compulsory technical schools were introduced were youths could learn skills such as woodcarving, needlework, cookery etc. during the evenings for the 'great benefit of all classes'. Working men had an opportunity to 'better themselves' from 1833 with the founding of a Reading Room and Literary Institute in the back parlour of Thomas Simmons, a printer and stationer and father of Sydney Simmons, the great Okehampton benefactor. In 1857, the Institute was moved to the Town Hall where a Reading Room was established.

In 1834, the work of the parish overseers was taken over by a new board or 'union' system, which brought the responsibilities of several parishes together under one body. The Okehampton Union was formed in 1834 and covered twenty-eight parishes. Four years later saw the opening of the Union Workhouse along Castle Lane (*44*). This was designed to accommodate no fewer than two hundred and thirty 'inmates' consisting of paupers, orphans, 'lunatics', elderly and infirm of the town and district with the principle that they should earn their keep where possible. It was also a way of discouraging the 'undeserving' from claiming relief in the first place of course. The giving of 'out-relief' to the able-bodied pauper was discouraged in favour of 'in-maintenance' where a man would have to bring his whole family into the workhouse and so become subject to its, often harsh, rules. It thus became seen as a place of last resort and did little to tackle the root causes of poverty and hardship. The elected guardians were drawn from among the local gentry, clergy and yeomen, voted into office by the district's ratepayers. The paid staff included two relieving officers, a clerk, a schoolmistress and a master and porter who both lived on the premises.

Under the laws of settlement, relief was generally charged to the parish in which paupers last slept. This did little to encourage mutual support or 'care in the community'! There is a local tradition explaining an anomaly on the boundary between Bridestowe and Sourton parish and Okehampton Hamlets (which became a parish in its own right under the Local Government Act of

1894) which could be accounted for by the settlement laws. An odd, wedge-shaped, extension to the Hamlets extends to a spot known as Iron Catch Gate on the open common to the east of Sourton Tors. It stands on the route of the old King Way high road between Tavistock and Okehampton. The story goes that the body of a traveller was once found on this wild and windswept heath but the parishes of Bridestowe and Sourton, on whose common it lay, refused to take responsibility for burying him. It therefore fell to the neighbouring parish of Okehampton to collect his body and lay him to rest in the churchyard of All Saints and, henceforth, they have always laid claim to the place where he fell. Who this anonymous traveller was and how Iron Catch Gate got its name when there are no walls, let alone a gateway, in sight, have been the subject of much speculation among local historians over the years. Incidentally, the northwest facing slopes of Sourton Tor was once the site of an ice works, making good use of the bitter winter winds that strike this exposed location. In the 1880s, spring water was channelled into trenches and allowed to freeze before being cut out and packed into a well-insulated icehouse where it would be kept until spring for distribution to the coastal fishing industry. The enterprise was somewhat short-lived however, as much of the cargo used to melt in transit.

Talking of walls and commons, this was the era of enclosures and attention had again turned to Dartmoor's barren slopes for what they might offer the speculator. In an age when people like 'Turnip' Townsend and more locally, Sir Thomas Tyrwhit, the founder of Princetown, had been experimenting with improving soils, crop rotations and the breeding of more hardy stock, attempts were even made by speculators to enclose vast expanses of the commons of northern Dartmoor. In one case around the turn of the nineteenth century, a Scotsman, named Matthew Crawford, employed gangs of Irish labourers to construct a dry-stone wall across neighbouring Belstone common. They worked, many of them bare-footed, for weeks while the commoners stood by and watched with indignation. When the task was finally complete the commoners hit back, fists flew and the wall was breached in so many places that its builders withdrew for good along with their employer! An old moorland saying goes "You scratch my back and I'll slit your purse" and so it was for many such ventures down the years. Among the more enduring changes though, was the introduction of hardier breeds of sheep and cattle from Scotland and the north of England later in the century, enabling commoners to keep stock out on the open moor year round. Improved roads and communications, together with the more general introduction of wheeled carts, improved ploughs and implements and even mechanical threshing machines on the wealthier farms slowly changed the centuries old pattern of highly labour intensive, subsistence farming around the moor's fringe. In spite of these gradual improvements, prices for produce were low and agriculture went through a very difficult period around the middle of the century. Many left the land to seek employment in towns or, more drastically, emigrated to Australia or the Americas to start afresh. Not that town life was any better for some. The 1851 census records almost one hundred paupers living in the parish and another one hundred and eighty in the workhouse.

Fore Street looking east in around 1880, following the demolition of most of Middle Row. Mount Ribbon is still standing against the tower of St. James and Gayer's House is to its right. (Museum of Dartmoor Life)

Many of the town's buildings were empty or in a state of decay and most of the old burgage plots had long since been in-filled with slum-type courtyards, packed with small cottages and workshops, often lacking the most basic sanitary arrangements. Some of the ramshackle buildings of Middle Row were already being pulled down for safety and fire was still a constant problem, despite the continued ringing of the curfew bell. In 1855, Charles Kingsley, in his famous novel *Westward Ho!* described Okehampton as an 'ugly, dirty and stupid town… in which fallen man (by some strange perversity) has chosen to defile one of the loveliest spots in the pleasant land of Devon'. Conditions in the old town lock-up were even worse than those of the workhouse. A report of 1803 had described it as consisting of :–

> 'two rooms about 12 feet by 7, dark and dirty. In the lower room a privy. Each has an iron grating that looks towards the street. A bundle of straw, weekly, is supplied when wanted. Formerly debtors were kept in the upper room. Nineteen prisoners have been confined here at a time, for a night or two. No water. No courtyard.'

A new police station and cells were built a little way up High Street towards the end of the nineteenth century and the County constabulary took over responsibility for keeping her Majesty's peace from the town constables.

There were genuine attempts to improve things as the century wore on and Queen Victoria came to the throne. After the neglect of the early part of the century, interest in the church affairs had picked up and St. James Chapel came back into use, the Sunday Schools thrived and the first purpose-built Wesleyan Methodist chapel was constructed in 1841 (*45*). The following year was to see disaster strike the parish church however. It had been re-seated at some considerable cost and the dilapidated gallery removed. Albany Savile had given a fine organ which was placed in a loft in the tower along with a stove to air and keep it dry but, alas, this gift was to cost the church dear. In the early afternoon of February 13th, 1842, it somehow caught the church alight and within an hour, despite the best efforts of the townsfolk with the fire engine and chains of buckets, it had destroyed the entire building, save for the fifteenth century tower. Rev. Savile could only watch in horror and plead "Oh save my poor church!" as his father's gift went up in flames along with the venerable old building. The church was re-built shortly after by Hayward of Exeter for the sum of £3,160 6s. 2d. but most of the old monuments and fittings had been destroyed in the conflagration. Nevertheless, church life went on with renewed vigour thereafter and, with new lighting and heating, congregations swelled. In 1862, the nave of St. James Chapel too was re-built with provision for another aisle against the north wall should the need arise.

With the recent turnpike improvements, the tithe map of 1841 reveals a basic street much like that with which we are familiar today – with the exception of the two Middle Rows at either end of the main street of course. The frontages of the buildings on either side, however, looked totally different. The two old hump backed bridges had been replaced. West Bridge was re-built in 1831. Vokins, the architect who designed Oaklands Mansion was apparently

Late 19th century sketch of West Bridge by F. J. Widgery, showing the Methodist church and High Street beyond. (Okehampton Town Council)

responsible for the graceful structure, which, sadly, was eventually blown-up in 1957 to make way for a wider, re-aligned, road bridge. East Bridge was re-built in 1841 and widened in 1887.

With better communications, the town became less insular and self-sufficient and was opened up to new trade opportunities and competition. A trade directory of 1840 lists four saddlers, three coopers, three curriers, five boot and shoe makers, three millers, three maltsters, twelve inns and five teaching academies. Another of 1850 includes five blacksmiths, nine boot and shoemakers, eight carpenters, seven stonemasons, two straw-hat makers and five wheelwrights. Inward investment brought new industries also. Adventurers started to search for exploitable minerals in the rich and varied bands of metamorphic rock, which surrounded the granite mass. Copper, lead, tin, iron, arsenic, zinc, manganese and even silver were discovered in varying quantities. Speculators from both near and far invested large sums of money. Farmers and landowners were especially keen to have rich seams discovered beneath their land and to receive the kind of royalties enjoyed by the Duke of Bedford from the famous Devon Great Consols Mine near Tavistock. Shaft mines were an expensive undertaking with no guarantee that workable veins would be encountered. Modern machinery and pumps powered by horses, water or, less commonly in this area, steam beam engines, were also costly so more fortunes were lost than gained in reality. There was even an attempt to develop a mine within the borough when the Okehampton Mine was opened between West Bridge and Lodge Bridge, on Squire Holley's land. The first turves were cut amid high hopes and great celebrations in 1864. The town band played and a barrel of beer was broached for the miners and assembled crowd to drink to its future. In the event, like most ventures of its kind, it was short lived and there are no records of any ore being produced. There were other failed attempts within the parish near the castle, by the East Okement below Halstock and at Wigney, two miles to the south west of the town. Among those in the district that did achieve some success were Ramsley copper mine, near South Zeal, which reached a depth of 200 fathoms (365m) and produced over 10,000 tons of ore between 1850 and 1909.

Skilled miners came from Cornwall, Wales and Ireland to seek employment alongside local men, whose knowledge of Dartmoor mineral bearing rocks was much sought after. In spite of their skills, wages and conditions weren't good. Boys as young as ten worked underground and accidents, illness and premature death were common among miners due to the dangerous work in the damp, cramped tunnels with poor ventilation. So too were lung diseases caused by dust, especially among arsenic miners and the men who scraped the arsenic dust from the walls of calciners with only sacking over exposed skin and handkerchiefs over their mouths and noses for protection. Miners often had to walk several miles to remote mines early on a Monday morning, carrying enough basic food for the week, and spend eight or nine hour shifts working underground by candlelight before climbing ladders back to the surface and warm bunks, freshly vacated by the next shift. They wouldn't then return home to their families until the following Saturday afternoon. Women and children too were sometimes employed in surface operations such as sorting and dressing ore.

The area around the small hamlet of Meldon was once a veritable hive of industry due to a unique concentration of minerals across the mile wide band of metamorphic (altered) rocks adjoining the Dartmoor granite. These included pockets of limestone, veins of copper and a fine aplitic rock, known locally as granulite. Limestone was quarried and burnt at Meldon from the eighteenth century. Copper was mined beneath the West Okement valley at Forest Mine (now under Meldon Reservoir) and at the Blackdown Copper Mine (also known as Devon Copper Mine and Okehampton Wheel Friendship). The granulite was quarried extensively and used for a while in glass making trials during the 1880s and 1920s. In the end, this went the same way as so many other optimistic local ventures. Of far greater success, however, was the hornfels quarry nearby. This extremely hard rock was discovered in 1874 during construction of the great iron railway viaduct, which still spans the valley. Its qualities and potential as railway ballast were immediately recognised and the London and South Western Railway Company opened a quarry in 1895. The extensive industrial remains of the Meldon valley are well worth exploring and feature leats (artificial water courses) a dry reservoir, waterwheel pits, adits (mine tunnels) and various ruined buildings including two lime kilns. Care must be taken however as such remains and quarry faces can obviously be dangerous. A splendid view of the valley can be afforded from the top of the now disused viaduct, which has been opened for the enjoyment of walkers and cyclists. The viaduct itself is quite a feat of engineering. It was originally built of wrought iron, in 1874, to carry a single track across the West Okement valley at 950 feet (290 m) above sea level – the highest stretch of line in the south of England. It was widened in 1879, with the addition of a steel girder lattice construction, to take a second track. The rocking of carriages by gusting cross-winds funnelling down through the valley must have been an unnerving experience for passengers as they crossed the slender structure of the earliest viaduct!

Many of the hand tools required for the mines, quarries and farms of the district were produced by the Finch family at their edge tool manufactory in Sticklepath – commonly known as Finch Foundry although, technically, a forge. Three water wheels powered the ingenious range of machinery, the earliest of which (a pair of tilt or trip hammers) was installed, second hand, in the former fulling mill, by William Finch in 1814. Incredibly, much of it can still be seen working and is now maintained by the National Trust having been saved by descendants of the Finch family after it finally closed in 1960. An iron foundry, making larger farm implements, grills and manhole covers, was established off Market Street (formerly Lodge Road) in Okehampton by James Glass around the turn of the twentieth century.

Charles Geen established a furniture making business by East Bridge in 1869, Gunn's Mineral Water Works and bottling plant was started in Kempley Road in 1896, moving to East Street in 1910. Thomas Day latched on enthusiastically to the advent of the motor car, leasing the old Methodist Chapel in New Road and opening a garage where he even made motorcycles and assembled car kits. T.F. Wood's chemical manure works were set up near the old Town Mills in Mill Road and W.B. German established a boot factory on the site of the old Clapps Mill above Lodge Bridge in the 1890s. He went

The scene in Fore Street in August 1871 when the opening of the railway was celebrated with a great tea party. A triumphant evergreen arch was built at the far end and trees were temporarily planted on either side especially for the occasion. (Museum of Dartmoor Life)

on to replace the two water wheels with turbines and eventually erected a purpose-built factory on the site, employing a large number of people. Larger scale manufacturing industries had arrived at last but, by then, so to had the railway and with it came increased competition from mass-produced imports. But at the same time it provided a means of exporting manufactured goods and farm produce to much bigger markets, thereby creating wealth and employment. It also enabled the import of cheaper raw materials and consumer goods not available in the district previously.

The arrival of the railway was to have profound implications for most people. For the first time they could travel long or short distances with relative ease and at a price all but the poorest of society could afford. In so doing, it broadened individual horizons in an unprecedented way. It also provided an opportunity to attract tourists to enjoy the wild beauty of northern Dartmoor and the picturesque towns and villages that surrounded it. Not surprisingly, the opening of the London South Western Railway's standard gauge line from Exeter in August 1871 was greeted with scenes of great jubilation in the town. A great tea party was arranged in Fore Street, by then bereft of most of the old Middle Row. There were three rows of trestle tables, running the full length of the street, with an evergreen triumphant arch at the western end, bunting fluttering in the breeze and small trees placed temporarily along either side to add to the colour of the occasion. The 'navvies' who had worked so hard on its construction were given pride of place in the feast that ensued to the accompaniment of the town band. Within three years, the line had been extended to Lydford Junction, where it met with the rival Great Western Railway Company's broad gauge line from Tavistock and Plymouth. Eventually the LSWR followed a separate route to its own Tavistock North Station and built a branch line from Meldon Junction to the North Cornwall coastal resort of Bude, opening as far as Holsworthy by 1879 but not reaching its final destination until 1898.

The new railway link also attracted the interest of the War Office who had long recognised the potential of the Dartmoor's vast open spaces for military training and now found it within easy reach. An early attempt occurred in 1873 when a whole army corps took part in manoeuvres on the southern moor. Over 12,000 men and 2,100 horses were involved. It wasn't all plain sailing however. The scale of the operation, coupled with bad weather and unexpected difficulties with the terrain, soon led to problems. Horses got trapped in bogs, wagons broke on boulders and whole units became lost in the mists. One regiment, which marched in the wrong direction, "was fortunately met by a civilian who happened to be carrying a pocket compass"! This didn't deter the officers and men who pitched their tents on Halstock Down, just south of Okehampton, in 1875 for three weeks of artillery practice. On this occasion things went rather better and the War Office decided to build a permanent camp, taking out a 999 year lease from the Duchy of Cornwall on a large tract of north Dartmoor. Okehampton Artillery Camp was built between 1892 and 1894 with accommodation for 200 men and stabling for 760 horses. A small permanent staff was supplemented during the training season by a gun battery, which ran the ranges. Special military sidings were constructed near the station to cope with the regular arrivals and departures of artillery units and equipment.

The second half of the nineteenth century saw great improvements to the standard of housing and sanitation in the town and the introduction of first gas street lighting in 1859. The Okehampton Gas Company works were sited on the south bank of the East Okement, about 500m upstream of East Bridge. The town's entrepreneurs were quick to grasp new opportunities with enthusiasm. Charles Geen installed the first electricity generating plant in the west country at his joinery works above East Bridge in 1880. By 1885, it was supplying other businesses in the vicinity with 100 volts, DC power, generated by a 16HP water turbine and supplemented by an 8HP steam engine, fuelled by wood shavings from the firm's sawmills. It was distributed to several shops and inns for lighting via copper-cored cable in a wooden sheath and cost 4d. (2p) a unit. The plant was replaced in 1899 by a 150HP engine and a large battery of accumulators as more people recognised the value of the new commodity and demand grew. Geen and his brother, Henry, were also instrumental in the regeneration of the town through various building projects including The Arcade, which was loosely modelled on London's Burlington Arcade. Henry Geen commenced the project with the Fore Street entrance in 1894. The southern entrance, with its ornate terracotta and wrought iron work, was completed in 1900 and it has provided a wide range of shops, a popular meeting place and a welcome refuge from Okehampton rain ever since.

The Geen brothers, Paltridges, Blatchfords and various other local builders transformed the appearance of the town centre between them in a wave of optimism for the future. Sadly though, many of the quaint and interesting old buildings were swept away by the changes too, leaving only faded photographs and rose-tinted memories as evidence that they ever existed. A few still survive behind Victorian or Edwardian facades and the occasional low and narrow slate-clad frontage offers a glimpse of what went before. It is hard now to imagine the two narrow streets with their ramshackle, tight-packed shops and houses which preceded today's wide thoroughfare with its symmetrical lines and large, illuminated shop signs. Anything more than a casual look, however, will reveal some quite pleasing architectural details and decoration as the legacy of these Victorian visionaries. Alas though, one has to resort to photographs and memories once again to discover the classic Victorian lines of Seth Harry's famous grocery shop – still remembered fondly by many older Oketonians and country folk. This imposing building was itself demolished to make way for the new International Store in 1968. Many new houses were built to accommodate workers and a number of 'villas' were constructed towards the station for better-off families and to provide accommodation for the increasing number of visitors to the 'gateway to Dartmoor'. Okehampton was even promoted as a health resort on account of the clean and bracing air it offered.

In 1889 the local historian, W.H.K. Wright, confidently wrote that "The stigma attaching to the town in Kingsley's time has been removed and the place is as pleasant, clean and enlightened as any little market town of its size and importance in the British Isles. Many handsome villas have been erected in and around the town by the enterprise of some of the local builders, and the principal shops in the main street would be no disgrace to many larger towns." The old Borough charter was surrendered following the passing of the Municipal Act of 1882 and, in line with the general mood of optimism and change, a new municipal borough charter of incorporation was granted in 1885. This allowed for properly elected members for the first time and virtually anyone could stand (as long as they were over twenty one and male however). The new Borough Council invested a great deal of money in re-paving the streets, introducing a mains water supply from a small reservoir at Bracken Tor above the town and a proper drainage scheme to go with it. They were also at pains to re-develop the market site to encourage more trade and rents. First, a new pannier market (named after the baskets used to bring produce in) was built in 1880 to replace the 'rickety old shanties with their pebbled gangway open to the sky' (this was replaced in turn by the present Charter Hall in 1973). The surviving Market Hall was built in 1900, seven years after the adjoining two-storey 'Technical Schools' block. Meanwhile, responsibility for St. James Chapel had passed to Charity Trustees in 1873, a move that the Corporation disapproved of however. At the turn of the twentieth century, the advent of a particularly high church vicar as chaplain gave rise to a dispute between the Church and some of the Trustees. As a result, a new chapel, dedicated to St. John, was built in Market Street (on the site of the present Church Hall) and services were held there instead. With an increasing volume of motor traffic entering the town, it was even suggested that St. James should be demolished to widen the thoroughfare. Fortunately the differences were settled before such drastic and irreversible action was taken.

The town's population remained at around the 2,000 mark for much of the latter half of the century, swelling to 2,500 around 1870 when the railway was being built. By the turn of the century it was on the increase though; from 1,879 in 1891 to 2,569 in 1901 and 3,174 in 1911. The opposite was true in the rural district around Okehampton, however, as depopulation gathered pace with increasing farm mechanisation and changing needs and aspirations among the young. The great estates and the ties that went with them were in decline also. Major General Holley, a man of forthright Conservative politics, had acquired Oaklands in 1898 and became prominent in local politics in the early years of the twentieth century, though, unlike his predecessor to the squire's title, Albany Savile, he didn't always get his way. As contemporary newspaper cuttings will testify, local political debate was rather heated at times and the night of a parliamentary election count or local election results would witness scenes of immense excitement and intense passions. Results were usually announced from the balcony of the White Hart Hotel to large and noisy crowds. For all his efforts to maintain the old ways, Holley represented the end of an era. His son and heir allegedly lost much of the estate through gambling but the labour shortages and political changes brought about by the First World War were to spell the end for many country estates – including Oaklands. A few years afterwards, the mansion was sold to clear debts and was being converted into luxury flats when it mysteriously caught alight and much of the opulent interior was gutted – the final indignity to Savile's grandiose designs.

EDWARDIAN DREAMS

It was Christmas Eve at last and Dora sat gingerly on the crackling bundle of sticks upon the fire in the parlour and made her wish in the customary way. She had no idea what the future held, everything in the old town and the world at large seemed to be changing so quickly that the possibilities seemed endless. Her full name was Dora Emilie Weekes and she had just turned sixteen *(46)*.

The family of Dora Weekes in about 1898. Left to right, Flora Jane, William, Elsie, Dora, Tom, Ada Jane and Flora (Floss)

She lived with her parents, Tom and Flora Jane Weekes above her father's saddler's shop at 12 Fore Street, together with her elder sisters, Ada Jane, Flora (Floss) and Elsie. Her elder brother, William, was a trained chemist and had recently gone to join his uncles who were chemists in London. Dora had left school just over a year before and now worked in the neighbouring draper's shop of T.C. Westcott. The year was 1909 and life for a teenage girl in Edwardian Okehampton was bright and happy – even exciting at times. Family ties and a loving home were sufficient to keep her from wanting to follow in her brother's footsteps although she missed him and loved to hear of his exploits in the big metropolis whenever he wrote or visited. Her father was a saddler by trade, having trained in London himself, but he was really a farmer at heart. He kept some ponies and sheep on the commons and made full use of the long yard, with its range of outbuildings and stables, at the back of the house and a vegetable garden that stretched down to the river Okement. The rambling old house had very thick walls and long passages on all three floors. Her mother had to work hard to keep it up but was helped with the household chores by a live-in maid called Hetty, whom she had trained herself and was treated like one of the family.

The shop smelt of leather and saddle soap and this also permeated through to the dark little parlour behind. Dora was very proud of her father's skill and had always been taken by the model of a white horse in the shop window, fitted with a miniature set of harness that he had made to demonstrate his skills. He had to work hard for the little money he made from the business but the family managed between them. Ada helped with the paperwork and Floss, who was good at needlework, would make dresses for the family and mend her father's clothes. She also helped in the house and worked for the two ladies who ran the Temperance Hotel across the street. The evils of the demon drink and the virtues of honest hard work had been drummed into the girls from childhood through church and Sunday School as well as from the formidable schoolmistresses at the Council School. Dora's sister Elsie was a born teacher herself. She had taught young Hetty to read and write and was now training at Exeter University to become a fully qualified teacher.

Dora had mixed memories of her own school days. She recalled the neat rows of desks in the high classrooms of the Council School and the hours spent chanting out tables or scratching practice letters and sums on slates; the smells of freshly starched frocks and disinfectant, the poor starving wretches who shared the classroom and playground and the ever-present fear of corporal punishment. Play times provided welcome relief and she loved playing with a hoop or at hopscotch or tag and even the boys' marbles and conkers if she got the chance! Still, she had not been too sorry when she left to attend a small private school at Mayville in Fairplace and was able to develop her interests with the encouragement of the mistress there. Her brother William had attended the Grammar School at Tavistock, travelling there by train each day. Grammar school places weren't available for girls however and, like her sisters, Dora had finished her schooling at a boarding school called Seaton House in Plymouth. Although she had hated being away from home for such long periods, she realised how lucky she was too have such an education and how hard her parents had to work to provide it.

Generally, women in this part of the world still weren't encouraged to learn any more than purely domestic tasks nor to play any active part in society, let alone follow careers – other than teaching and nursing. Dora didn't have any particular ambitions herself though and, like most people in the town, her family didn't hold with the activities of Mrs. Pankhurst and friends, even

The Royal Horse Artillery parading through Fore Street in 1894 on their way to the Battle Camp. (Museum of Dartmoor Life)

though there might have been some sympathy for their cause. Dora would be happy to meet a handsome soldier and, perhaps, get the chance to see some of the exotic places she had read and dreamt about. The arrival of a fresh troop of soldiers, on their way to the army camp for artillery practice, was still a cause for much excitement for Dora and her friends and they would often run out to see them parade through Fore Street in their full dress uniforms. The buckles, buttons and braid on their smart red uniforms glinted in the sun, along with the shining brass on the horse harnesses and gun carriages. Even the toes of their boots glistened like mirrors – Dora thought they must have spent half of their time polishing – poor things! However dashing they may have looked, she knew that it was all a bit of a show really as, in reality, they descended from the Military sidings via the back streets and then paraded through the town centre before climbing Station Road and back to the Battle Camp. Dora's friends had often giggled about how they had hidden in the bushes by the sidings and watched the men in their 'long johns' as they changed into their dress uniforms on the platform after disembarking! Not that boys were much better. William had once had to tell Floss, who was a bit of 'tom boy' then, not to climb trees because his friends could see her drawers!

Okehampton had its own military hero in 'Sharpshooter' William Thomas Ward, a volunteer Private in the Devonshire Regiment. He was a carriage builder by trade but also a crack shot. He had won numerous prize medals for shooting competitions, including the gold medal at Bisley in 1897 and 1900 (*47*). He used to display them all over his uniform with great pride but wasn't seen around so much since his wife was killed in a tragic accident when boiling turpentine in his workshop, poor man. Unfortunately accidents were all too common in the home and workplace. Young children were easily drowned in the rivers and mill leats – they were dangerous play places and, with few safety guards or regulations to protect workers, terrible accidents sometimes occurred on farms and in the factories and mills of the district. Fires were still common also. Whenever the alarm was raised, the volunteers were mustered at the Market Hall while horses were procured to tow the appliance. Sometimes they were the well-groomed carriage horses from General Holly's stables at Oaklands but, more often than not, they had to be unhitched from the Borough Council's dustcart. The crew, with their shining brass helmets, then climbed aboard the smart red tender and clung onto the side rails for dear life while one rang the bell furiously. They would race off like Roman charioteers to the rescue of some poor soul whose thatched roof had been set alight by sparks from their hearth.

The curfew bell on the tower of St. James was still rung each evening at eight o'clock as a signal to extinguish fires. This also acted as a signal for children to go home after playing in the streets. As a girl, Dora was usually tucked up in bed by then but would sometimes peep out of the window to see what was going on as dusk fell on the town. Some friends were less well-behaved and apt to play truant from school on occasions. They would occupy their time playing by the river, scrumping apples from other peoples' orchards or collecting bird's eggs from the woods. On one occasion a boy had been caught in General Holly's grounds pinching ducks' eggs. When challenged, he quickly stuck the egg he was holding under his cap and claimed that he had only been trying to find his grandmother's cat that she loved so dearly. At first the old gamekeeper fell for his sad tale, until he gave the little rascal a sympathetic pat on the head. The game was soon up and the boy was literally left with egg on his face (*48*)!

Fortunately serious crime was still a rarity in these parts though. With everyone knowing everyone else's business it didn't usually take long to find the culprit. There had been great excitement three years before when, in a daring robbery, burglars had broken into Mr. Cornish's jewellery shop, just a couple of doors along from Dora's home, and got away with a suitcase full of loot. What a fright the girls had had knowing that they were so close while they lay asleep in their beds. For all their daring, the robbers didn't anticipate getting lost during their getaway or the efficiency of the local constabulary in tracking them down, nor the keen eyes of local hero, Simon Newcombe. He happened to be passing the shop on his way to catch the 9.13 train to Exeter that Sunday morning in September and, seeing the door open, had popped in to see if Mr. Cornish could look at his broken watch. On hearing of the break-in he said he would keep an eye out for the well-dressed strangers noticed around the town during the previous day. Meanwhile, Sergeant Beer of Okehampton Police Station had sent a telegram ahead to his colleagues in Crediton, Exeter and Plymouth to be on the look out while a constable was dispatched to check the up-bound train before it left. Mr. Newcombe caught this same train and spotted the suspects getting on at Sampford Courtenay. He watched them closely and followed them when they alighted at Exeter St. Davids. However, they noticed him and tried to give him the slip by going into the Railway Hotel. He then ran up to the Police station to alert them. Officers were dispatched including Detective Constable Shutler who spotted them on his way down to St. Davids, struggling up the hill with

Members of the Devon Constabulary investigate the robbery at Cornish's jewellery shop in Fore Street in 1906. (Museum of Dartmoor Life)

their case full of swag. He managed to follow them without being spotted and actually jumped into their open-topped, horse-drawn cab and, when they refused to open the case, ordered the driver to take them all to the Police Station rather than Pinhoe Railway Station as they wished. After some resistance, Mr. Simmons and another plain-clothed detective arrived and got into the cab with them. The cabby, a Mr. Endacott, pretended to go along with the villains but really was driving them all to the police station. There they where greeted by such a reception committee that they had no choice but to open the case which was found to contain a loaded revolver, the tools of their 'craft' and almost £1,000 worth of gold jewellery and watches!

They were escorted under close guard back to Okehampton on the following Monday to face the magistrates at the Town Hall. Large crowds gathered at the station and in the town to get a glimpse of the burglars. People queued for hours to get a place in the public gallery. They were greeted like celebrities when they eventually arrived in the town, especially by the children. They even smiled and waved at the crowds, including some that chose more discreet vantage points from behind their lace curtains above the street level. They were even interviewed by a reporter from the local newspaper and had a face-to-face meeting with Mr. Cornish, the jeweller, to whom they apologised and he responded "Well, it's done now". The two men were down from London and had planned their robbery and getaway pretty well but, for some reason, had lost their bearings and their escape had been slowed, hence their capture. The younger man, Harry Ross, alias Groves, who later became known in London as the 'king of the burglars', only got fifteen months imprisonment with hard labour on account of his remorse and it being the first offence of this kind. His older accomplice, James Long, got six years, however, because of his bad record. The policemen involved and Simon Newcombe were congratulated for their effective and brave actions not only by the magistrates but also by the burglars. It was indeed a 'fair cop gov'!

A fair amount of interest had also been aroused when the Prince of Wales' beautiful motor car had been garaged overnight at Mr. Day's in New Road, especially amongst the children. In fact it had not been so long ago that any motor car entering the town had been greeted with great excitement. Their drivers would often repay the interest with a 'honk, honk' on the horn and give a friendly wave, well, most of them! Some were a bit protective over their precious 'horseless carriages' and the last thing they wanted were lots of children following them along and getting smeary finger prints all over the gleaming body work and shining carriage lamps when they stopped. Dora's father had greeted them with a mixture of scepticism and concern. After all, the development of the internal combustion engine posed a threat to the dominance of the horse in both transportation and farm work and could have a serious affect on business if they ever became more affordable.

There were some amazing things happening in the world at large however. As the family sat around the fire in the evening, reading or sewing by the light of candles and an oil lamp, Tom would often read aloud from the newspaper about the latest scientific discovery or ingenious invention that was set to transform the way they lived. It was just seven years since the Wright brothers had made their historic first flight in an aeroplane and the previous year Monsieur Bleriot had flown right across the English Channel. The telephone and electricity were being introduced into more and more homes as well as businesses. Now experiments were being carried out which might one day allow people to hear music and speech from the other end of the country from the comfort of their own armchair – without the wires required by the telephone. For added entertainment, in many larger towns and cities, it was now possible to go to a picture house and see moving pictures projected onto a big screen to the accompaniment of an orchestra or pianist. New labour-saving gadgets were being designed and sold to make housework that little bit easier. There had also been some important developments in medicine, health care and welfare. Even though the effects on Dora's own life were slow in coming, the promise and anticipation of better things to come made it feel like the dawn of a new age. The old curfew bell was rung whenever anyone passed away in the parish, followed by the appropriate number of tolls for their age. With the advancements in medicine and improved health care, she hoped that the Sexton would have to labour long and hard when her time eventually came!

Some things never seemed to change however, especially hard work and struggling to make ends meet. Tom had always given the children a penny (0.5p) a week each as pocket money, in spite of his meagre income, and they had thought it was riches. It would buy a bar of chocolate or a bag of sweets for a treat but they would always save some for their parents. Their grandfather always gave them sixpence (2.5p) between them when he visited. He'd tell them to buy a penny stamp each from the Post Office and stick it on a sheet. When they'd collected twelve they would hand the form in again and have a shilling (5p) put into their savings books for a 'rainy day'. The other penny would buy a bag of sweets, which they'd share out between them. Sundays were a special day and as little work as possible was done because it was the Sabbath day. Dora had become a Sunday School teacher and there were lots of classes and organisations in the town, which encouraged Bible reading, temperance and good Christian values. When they were children, the girls and William would attend Sunday School at the Vicarage and then proceed to church for the eleven o'clock service. They all had to sit quietly on the north side, facing the children from the workhouse, in their uniforms, on the other. The Sexton would watch over them sternly and had a long rod to keep them in order. Their father was sidesman and William, who was in the choir, would pull faces at them sometimes but Mother would keep them in order and shake her head disapprovingly if any of them misbehaved. After church, they would often all squeeze into Father's jingle and ride off to see his sister, Aunt Polly, at her farm near Lewdown and then sing all the way home! They all looked forward to such outings with eager anticipation.

All the girls had been taught to ride side-saddle by their father and Dora loved riding up onto Dartmoor with him to round up ponies or sheep. Another favourite occupation was whort' picking on the moors in August. The juicy whortleberries (bilberries) grew in profusion on the more rocky hillsides and crowds would go out to pick them for pie making or selling at Newton Abbot market for the die trade. They were worth roughly sixpence (2.5p) per quart and on a good day a man could pick up to twenty quarts. Ten shillings (50p) was quite a lot of money for a day's work back then and, with the whole family out picking, it brought in some welcome extra cash. More importantly, to most of the children, it was the nearest thing they got to a holiday, with picnic hampers full of pies and buns wrapped in muslin cloth, jugs of cold tea, the beautiful views and the dainty sound of the skylarks on the warm breeze. It was like Heaven to Dora and she wished she could paint the atmosphere. She enjoyed painting and took great pleasure in studying the smallest details of garden and wild flowers and trying to capture them on paper. She would spend hours down by the river at the bottom of the garden reading, painting or just contemplating. It was so peaceful and beautiful down there. There were always animals for company though. Dad bred Collie dogs and there were two house cats that she loved. They were so gentle and one would even jump onto her bed in the morning and lift her eyelid with its paw to wake her. She loved animals and in her heart of hearts she would be happy to forego the romantic appeal of marrying a soldier and find a caring farmer instead.

Dora vaguely remembered the heroes' welcome given to men returning from the Boer War at the turn of the century and tales of their exploits seemed quite thrilling to an impressionable child but she had little concept of the harsh realities of war. In spite of the peace and relative prosperity enjoyed by Great

Britain since, there were tensions afoot in Europe, which worried her father. He maintained a keen interest in local politics and often got hot under the collar about the latest goings on in the Council Chamber. There were frequent heated debates, reflecting the political turmoil and conflicts between conservative and radical viewpoints at national level. Both local and general elections were fiercely contested and the atmosphere in the town in the run-up to and following the announcement of the results was highly charged, with near riots breaking out between the supporters of either side on occasions.

The town certainly knew how to celebrate. Dora could also just remember the great bonfire on East Hill that marked Queen Victoria's Diamond Jubilee in 1897 and the pomp and ceremony in the town that surrounded King Edward's coronation, following her death in 1901. The whole district appeared to have turned out in their Sunday best to listen to the bands and speeches. A similar occasion was enjoyed on 8th July 1907 with the opening of the new park by Sir

Major General Holley of Oaklands Mansion (standing) with his chauffeur prepare to drive the Lord Mayor of London, Sir William Treloar (left) and his Sheriff, Sir William Dunn to open Simmons Park on 8th July 1907. (Museum of Dartmoor Life)

William Treloar, Lord Mayor of London. The beautiful riverside fields and woods had been bought by the Town Council two years before but the cost was generously re-paid by Mr. Sydney Simmons of Finchley, north London. He had then paid for and taken a great interest in the planning and laying-out of the new park with its ornamental fountains and waterfalls. He also provided a Swiss-style chalet, named after the Lord Mayor, for the park keeper and two houses for the poor of the town. When he came to open the park he stayed with General Holley, amidst the luxuriant surroundings of Oaklands Mansion. This must have seemed such a contrast to the modest cottage in which he had been born back in 1840, when his parents ran a printing business next to the White Hart Hotel in West Street (part of the cottage is still standing in the Museum courtyard). Mr. Simmons, General Holley and Sir William Treloar, accompanied by his Sheriff, Sir William Dunn, had joined the assembled guests and civic dignitaries from all over Devon that afternoon for the opening ceremony. A covered grandstand had been specially erected near the park entrance. In his speech, the Lord Mayor had said that his great friend, Sydney Simmons, 'not only had the brains to make money, but had the heart to spend it' and referred to his acts of kindness to his workers and their families back in London. Everyone was very proud of their 'local boy made good'. Even the torrential rain didn't dampen the enthusiasm of the assembled crowd of spectators, nor the children's appetite for the tea that followed!

Their elders and teachers did not waste the opportunity to point out what an excellent example he was to the children of the town then. He had gone away to school in Lincolnshire when he was only six or seven and had then taken up an apprenticeship with a Plymouth drapery firm before going to join a carpet manufacturing firm in London. While there, he had been inspired by the beautiful works of art and decorative objects from around the world in the South Kensington Museum, where he spent much of his leisure time. He had studied works on decoration, never dreaming that he would one day be able to study them first hand in the ruins of Pompeii, the temples of Egypt or the Alhambra in Granada. After seven years he became the company's representative in North America and thus began a life of travel and adventure. He had to work very hard to cover his expenses and make a living but, whilst in the USA, he acquired a patent for a carpet cleaning machine which he later developed in this country. Through his hard work and business acumen, he amassed a sizeable fortune but, clearly, never forgot his humble beginnings in Okehampton. He certainly made an impression on Dora, with his tidy white beard, smart suit and white Stetson hat and plenty of charm and charisma to match his distinguished appearance. She was totally riveted by the accounts of his many adventures on his travels around the world. These were recorded faithfully in the local newspaper after he had attended a banquet in his honour at the White Hart the previous year. The first journey he remembered was a trip to Exeter with his mother in a wagon drawn by three horses. They had left Okehampton at eight o'clock in the evening and didn't arrive until seven the next morning. How times had changed.

His first trip to America was on a steam ship to Boston in a record-breaking crossing of seven days and twenty two hours. His subsequent life of travel and adventure could have been equalled by very few alive in 1909. By his own account "I have been in accidents by rail and steamboat, and have had experiences in hotel fires as well as city fires. I have taken dinner in the mammoth caves of Kentucky, and have been on a steamboat that has stuck on the sawdust banks of the river Ottawa. I have smoked my pipe in the wigwam of a North American Indian, and have danced with Negroes on a Mississippi boat. I was nearly a week on an ice flow, surrounded by icebergs, on my way to Newfoundland. I have visited most of the towns on the Continent, have had a gamble at Monte Carlo, and fished in Norway; Switzerland I know almost as well as I know Dartmoor. I have been outside and inside of the pyramids of Egypt, have snapped caravans of camels on the way from Fez to Morocco, and the King of Spain and his mother in the park of Madrid. I have taken coffee with Arabs on the sand dunes of the great Sahara desert, but never felt so big, nearly eight feet high, as when I listened to the drums and fifes of His Majesty's Regiment coming down the narrow streets and echoing in the great Rock of Gibraltar". For these were the halcyon days of the British Empire.

Another occasion for celebration locally was the beating of the parish bounds. It only took place every seven years (*49*) and everyone from town and country would turn out to walk or ride around the moorland boundary of the Okehampton Hamlets parish. At each boundary stone, a parish elder would join with a young child and strike the stone with a stick while everyone chanted out the occasion and the name of the stone so that their location would long be remembered. The old custom of 'spurling' was still kept up and the boys seemed to find scrambling about in the bogs for apples as much fun as ever (though their mothers weren't so pleased with the state they get into!). Refreshments and sports were enjoyed at Halstock before everyone trudged home, happy but exhausted.

Recently, Okehampton had staged its first ever carnival to raise funds for the hospital and local charities and what a spectacle it was. Hundreds of spectators had flocked into the town to watch the colourful torchlight procession; consisting of some eighty entries, including twenty decorated tableaux, to the accompaniment of local bands. Individual entries were well dressed-up and mounted or on foot, many of them topical, including more than a couple of

'Suffragettes' and one entitled 'The Budget' making fun of the House of Lords' rejection of Mr. Lloyd George's budget. Elaborate wheeled tableaux depicted scenes including a hospital ward – complete with patients in beds, doctors and nurses; Britannia; a lifeboat and crew; a poaching scene and a beautiful 'State Coach', in which the carnival officials rode, complete with driver, outriders and mounted heralds – all in fine livery. Then there were trade tableaux demonstrating the work and products of various local industries and the smartly turned out Fire Brigade with their horse-drawn engine led by Capt. Newcombe. Prizes were awarded to the best entries by the Committee, the judges being members of the local gentry and respected doctors and lawyers. During the day, the crowds were able to enjoy the many side-shows laid on in the Butchers' Market including a confetti stall, concerts and refreshments, lightning sketches, a football shooting competition, hoop-la, a shooting gallery and boxing pavilion, 'Mephisto's Mysteries and Professor Skinflint's twentieth Century Wonders. During the afternoon and evening, Mr. Smale and Mr. Horwell went around the streets dressed in Italian costume and sang and played a piano to entertain the crowds while Mr. Coombe (the band master) and his party went around with a perambulator and accordion dressed as 'out of works'. From half past eight until one o'clock there was a dance and confetti fete in the Pannier Market which had been gaily festooned with flags and bunting. The grand finale to the evening was a spectacular fireworks display. Dora had gone home feeling quite giddy with the thrill of it all, the music and fireworks still ringing in her ears, and had fallen into bed and was asleep almost as soon as her head hit the pillow.

Of a slightly more serious note but equally enjoyable in its own way, was the annual agricultural show with its horsemanship events and livestock showing – another occasion when town met country. There was a great deal of earnest preparation and keen competition in the run-up to the judging of each class as the farmers and stockmen groomed their charges to perfection. Dora loved the side-shows and tents full of colourful produce, sweet smelling flowers and intricate crafts on show and there was plenty to interest her father among the livestock pens and trade stands where he took the opportunity to renew old acquaintances and to discuss business with clients. The annual show wasn't the only big occasion in the farming calendar. The regular Saturday markets saw the town alive with activity but the annual fair days in March and October had an atmosphere of their own. People would flock in from miles around to buy from the numerous stalls lining Fore Street with their sweetmeats, fruit, household items, fabrics, tinkers' wares and so on. The streets were not only packed with people. There were pens of sheep, horses, calves and long-horned cattle stretching right up through into East Street. The latter were quite a hazard and passers by had to be wary lest the beasts turned quickly and give them a nasty blow. There were steam-driven fairground rides like the beautiful Golden Gallopers to enjoy, accompanied by the jolly music of the fair organs and dances were held in the Market Hall to the accompaniment of a fiddler. The Great Market before Christmas was an especially popular occasion for the neighbouring farming communities and the colourful Giglet Fair on the first Saturday after Christmas, with its old customs and romantic overtones, was a particular favourite of farm labourers and youngsters of course.

This Christmas, was largely a family occasion as always. Dora remembered with fondness how, as children, they would wake excitedly on Christmas morning and run into each other's rooms shouting 'Merry Christmas!'. They each had a present and a stocking filled with nuts, an apple and orange and a bright new penny. But her favourite part of Christmas was still Christmas Eve. William was down from London and they were all sitting around the hearth in the parlour. The room was gaily decorated with evergreens and ribbons and the oil lamp was casting a warm glow on the surroundings. The family sang Christmas carols while the ginger and raison wine was passed around. Everyones' eyes seemed to be glittering and there was an air of anticipation when, suddenly, the door burst open and in came Tom's workshop assistant, Mr. Alford, with the traditional 'Ashen faggot' (a bundle of small sticks tied with ash bands). Tom ceremoniously placed it on the flames of the fire and a cheer went up. He summoned young Dora over and, with some apprehension she sat briefly upon the crackling bundle and made her wish as the tradition dictated. She had decided, she wanted to marry a farmer from the district and live to a ripe old age, close to the family she loved so dearly.

As each of the ash bands spit and burst, another cheer went up and the sweet drink was passed around. The future looked as rosy as her cheeks but would her wishes come true?

INTO THE MODERN AGE

Most of Dora's wishes did indeed come true. She married a farmer's son called William Endacott from Throwleigh in 1922 at the age of twenty eight and moved into Clannaborough Farm on his father's retirement. They had a daughter, Louie and a son, Tom – my father. Coincidentally, her dreams of marrying a soldier also came true as my grandfather was called up during the First World War and, because of his skills in horsemanship, served in the Royal Horse Artillery. My grandmother's brother, William, with his pharmacy training, served in the Royal Medical Corps throughout the Great War and helped hundreds of wounded soldiers before dying from shear exhaustion in March of 1918. Shortly before going back to the trenches in 1916, during a brief spell of home leave, he had married my grandfather's eldest sister, Louie. They were to be together for just one short week – a poignant example of the all too common human tragedy of the First World War. After the War, her father – my great grandfather – gave up the saddler's shop and moved to Parklands, Okehampton, from where he continued to run a smallholding. Grandma died in 1988, having attained the ripe old age of ninety four and maintaining her health and independence almost to the last. By then, however, the old curfew bell on St. James had long fallen silent, being last rung in the 1950s, so the Sexton was spared the task of tolling out her age!

The enormity of the changes that she and her generation experienced during their lifetime cannot be overstated. Wheeled vehicles of any description had barely been introduced to many isolated farms when she was born and even the journey to Exeter, which now takes half an hour in a car, then took a good half day. Although better-off townsfolk had basic sanitation and mains services laid-on by the turn of the twentieth century, those in more isolated areas continued to make do well into the second half of the century and mains electricity didn't reach many isolated farms and hamlets until the 1950s. Meanwhile, the space race was on, supersonic travel and instant global communication were becoming a reality, the computer age was in its infancy and that infamous square box in the living room was beginning to replace the wireless set as the new focus for family entertainment. Life in Okehampton was to change a little more slowly than that of big cities perhaps, but change it did. In 1911 an 'Electric Picture Palace' was opened in the Market Hall by an enterprising young man named Billy Ezard who had once worked as a cowboy on William Cody's ('Buffalo Bill') ranch in Wyoming before becoming one of his roughriders in his famous Wild West Circus. In fact, Billy would make a personal appearance in full cowboy attire on certain nights of the week! A permanent cinema was established opposite in 1915 when the Okehampton Picture Palace (later the Premier) was opened. The Carlton Cinema was opened in 1936. Together with the introduction of the wireless set to many households between the Wars, the new media broadened many individual horizons and aspirations. The still rather insular nature of this and many other rural communities was to change as a consequence leading to a much swifter introduction of new fashions and social influences, especially among the younger generation.

But it was the Great War of 1914-18, rather than new technology or fashion that was to be one of the greatest instruments of social change. The death or disablement of so many young men led to severe labour shortages on the district's farms and factory floors. Many women of marriageable age were unable to find husbands while many others were widowed and left to bring up young families with little support from the still infant welfare state. Times were very hard for many while there were some, no doubt, who profited from the shortages of the time. As junior officers were expected to lead from the front, many of the young gentry, who made up the officer classes during the War, failed to come back to take up their inheritance and the old squirearchy was never to recover from the tragedy. The political balance had changed also and the working classes were less inclined to simply accept the old system. Women too had at last won the right to vote and thus had a greater say in how society was run. During the War itself though, patriotism loomed large and much effort on the 'Home Front' was devoted to King and Country and supporting the soldiers and sailors of the Empire in their endeavours – both in a practical and moral sense.

However, there was generally little recognition of the true suffering and carnage from across the Channel, save for the harrowing accounts of returning servicemen or the dreaded black edged envelope bearing news of the loss of a loved one. One of the ways local women and children helped the War effort was by collecting large quantities of sphagnum moss from the commons for use as field dressings. Many of those who enlisted from the district were volunteers in the local company of the 6th Devonshire Regiment and fought together. Although this arrangement encouraged greater camaraderie, it ran the risk of virtually the whole male community of an area being wiped out in one action. The local Headquarters of the Regiment was the Drill Hall (now the Conservative Club) which was opened in 1914. Meanwhile General Holley's military experience and leadership skills came to the fore as he continued to wield considerable influence in the affairs of the town and corporation, though nothing like that of his predecessor, Albany Savile. He held various offices locally and was Mayor for five consecutive terms from 1913. But, like his predecessor, there was to be no lasting dynasty and his son disposed of much of the estate before, finally, selling the century old mansion and ninety four acres in the late 1920s. The house was also evidently run-down as it was advertised with the option of buying it with the land or separately for salvage materials following its demolition. Fortunately this was never carried out but during the course of the work to convert it into luxury flats in 1930, a mysterious fire broke out and the beautiful building was gutted. Luckily the shell survived however, and the house was renovated and is still occupied today. Talking of fires, four years earlier, the Fire Brigade themselves had suffered the embarrassment of having their engine destroyed by a blaze which started in a fish fryer in the Market cafe adjoining the Market Hall where it was kept!

The town recovered slowly after the Great War, though few of the promising industrial and commercial ventures of the turn of the century were to prosper. An attempt to re-open the granulite quarries at Meldon for glass making in 1920, for instance, was short-lived in spite of early optimism. A London-based syndicate purchased the quarry and introduced skilled glass workers from the continent to conduct trials and get the factory underway with a suitably trained local workforce which, it was anticipated, would eventually number over five hundred. Around a quarter of a million pounds capital was to be raised in order to construct twelve oil-fired furnaces, each with a capacity of 120 tons. Unfortunately though, the full scheme never came to fruition and the venture lasted little over twelve months. Even though the granulite mineral provided some eighty per cent of the raw materials required for the manufacture of glass, it proved very difficult to remove impurities, which caused a green tinge at a time when its aesthetic beauty was not so acceptable. Numerous light green bottles were produced alongside novelty or apprentice pieces such as ornamental smoking pipes and walking sticks – hardly the most practical of items! There are some examples in the Museum of Dartmoor Life. The granulite had for a time also been crushed and sold to Staffordshire porcelain manufacturers for enamelling and large reserves of this potentially valuable mineral had been identified. Sadly though, much of it ended up being used as road stone.

The LSWR ballast quarry at Meldon enjoyed its heyday between the wars, employing a large number of people. Gangs of men had to tunnel laboriously, at regular intervals, a hundred feet or so into the quarry face to lay the explosives that would bring another rich seem thundering down to be broken up manually into useable sizes. The work was hard and dangerous and accidents were common. The quarry is still operating and now covers an area of over one square mile. With the aid of modern explosives and massive machinery it now produces ten times as much material with only a tenth of the workforce. A smaller aggregate quarry on the northern outskirts of Okehampton is also still operating and was formerly the site of the Okehampton Brick Company, which was established in 1918. Quarry and farm labourers were among the main clients of German's boot factory, which continued to enjoy modest success with its 'celebrated Dartmoor Boot'. The original factory, in the converted Clapp's Corn mill between West Bridge and Lodge Bridge, was replaced by a purpose-built factory. The brick-built factory warehouse just above Lodge Bridge survived until the 1980s, when it was demolished to make way for a supermarket development. They also had a shop at the bottom of the Arcade and employed up to seventy people at one stage. This enterprise was to survive almost sixty years, eventually closing in 1950.

Similar success was enjoyed by the Devon Motor Transport Company (DMT) who took advantage of Okehampton's central position in the road network of Devon and Cornwall to build up, first a freight carrying operation and then, through a series of take-overs, a sizeable fleet of buses. These operated throughout the two counties from the Okehampton depot during the 1920s and employed up to two hundred people. They were subsequently bought out themselves, eventually becoming the famous Devon General Company, and the West Street depot was closed. Nearby stood the garage and engineering works of T. Day & Sons. They started off with a cycle shop in the Arcade but went on to manufacture cycles and assemble kit cars. They were a very progressive concern and boasted the first hydraulic tyre press in Devon for installing solid tyres, as well as designing and building engines to pull trucks along the five mile long Rattlebrook peat railway from Bridestowe Station to the remote works, high on the moors above. In spite of the remote and desolate location of the Rattlebrook peat beds, the West England Compressed Peat Company also employed a large number of people as attempts were made to successfully extract substances such as naphtha, acetic acid, tar oil and even alcohol and petroleum, from the spongy material. Though these operations were never perfected and the harsh climate scarcely made them easy, the works did continue for a number of years – bearing witness to the intrepid determination and spirit of generations of moormen. However, as the 'adventurers' were once again to find to their cost, the old Dartmoor saying "You scratch my back and I'll slit you purse" still held true.

Although various welfare acts gradually improved the lot of the least well off in society, charity and mutual support still played an important part. The generosity of the town's great benefactor, Sydney Simmons, continued unabated. He purchased and consolidated the castle ruins and passed them into the safekeeping of a specially established local trust in 1917 (*50*). He also gave the bowling green, played a major part in establishing the golf club and presented the Simmons Almshouses off Exeter Road. A sum of £10,000 given by him towards the building of a 'more fitting' town hall was eventually spent on renovating and extending the existing one in the 1960s. The Union Workhouse continued to operate as such until after the Second World War although conditions had been improved considerably in 1902, with better sanitation, the installation of fireplaces in the rooms, new laundry and kitchen facilities and opening sash windows in place of the old cell bars. Later, a new, purpose-built, cottage hospital was built next to the Simmons Almshouses, to commemorate those from the district who fell during the Great War, and the Workhouse building became the Castle Hospital for geriatric care. A new Police Station was built in George Street in to replace the one in High Street (*51*). Meanwhile, the numerous Okehampton charities were merged into two administrative trusts – the Ecclesiastical Trust, dealing with matters pertaining to the maintenance of the Church and St. James Chapel and the Non-Ecclesiastical Trust with the remit of benefiting the young people of the town and maintaining the Town Hall. Both Trusts still function although they have subsequently disposed of much of the vast amount of property they once possessed in the district and have invested the proceeds to derive an income.

The last vestiges of the ancient Middle Row were finally to fall victim to the motor car in the 1930s as the cottages and shops down the centre of West Street were demolished. The narrow lane to the rear that led down to the West Okement below West Bridge was called Rosemary Row. The main road through West Street was so narrow that it proved necessary to impose a five miles per hour speed limit as early as 1904. The area around the bridge was also prone to flooding and it was planned to re-build it at the same time but the Second World War intervened and the scheme wasn't completed until 1957. A similar situation existed in East Street and, among other buildings demolished was Mansion Court, with its imposing two-storey granite porch, which projected into the street. The dressed stones were numbered and stored with the intention of re-erecting the porch elsewhere but, once again the War interrupted the plans and the stones appear to have been lost. Meanwhile, the need for a 'by-pass' was already being discussed and plans were drawn-up in the 1930s for a route skirting around to the north, between the town centre and Oaklands. However, it was to be another fifty years before a bypass was actually built. Besides the noise of traffic, another new sound on streets of Okehampton was the Westminster chimes of the new clock which was installed in the tower of St. James Chapel to commemorate the Silver Jubilee of George V in 1935.

Fore Street looking west c. 1910. The White Hart Hotel can be seen on the left, the end of the West Street Middle Row with Rosemary Row to its right, the newly built Lloyds Bank building and the Town Hall. (Museum of Dartmoor Life)

Motorised vehicles and stationary engines gradually replaced the horse as the main source of power on the farms of the district too. The demise of horsepower was hastened during the Second World War by the drive for increased productivity when attacks on allied shipping convoys by U-boats and the Luftwaffe gave rise to food shortages at home. Tractors were also introduced on the artillery ranges between the wars, to pull the heavy gun carriages in place of horses. Spotter balloons were employed on the ranges from the late nineteenth century but it is perhaps hard to believe that the district once boasted an aerodrome given the hilly terrain in the vicinity. The Okehampton Aerodrome was situated on the ridge by Folly Gate, a couple of miles to the north of the town, and was established in the 1920s. Royal Air

Force squadrons occupied the aerodrome during the summer training season and worked in conjunction with the Royal Artillery at the Battle Camp on the opposite side of the valley, using gliders and light aircraft for spotter duties. The Aerodrome also received the Gypsy Moth aeroplane in which the Prince of Wales (later Edward VIII) arrived on his tour of Duchy property on Dartmoor on 28th May 1930 and played host to an impressive air display featuring ace flyer, Sir Alan Cobham in August 1932. Displays included aerobatics, air races, parachute descents, formation flying, aerial marksmanship, an autogiro and a grand flypast – before a large and enthusiastic crowd. There were opportunities to take scenic flights for as little as four shillings (20p), to have a flying lesson or even experience aerobatics first hand! All were accompanied by music transmitted over loud speakers to make it a truly memorable occasion. No doubt a few young men were encouraged to join the Royal Air Force themselves in order to get paid for the privilege of taking to the skies.

It wasn't long before the threat of war was looming on the horizon yet again though and the young men – and women – of the district were to be called to arms to defend King and Country once more. The scale of human sacrifice was sadly to be great again but this time the war was to come even closer to home. An orange glow in the night sky to the south and east of Okehampton bore witness to the terrible devastation wrought on Plymouth and Exeter during the 'blitz'. The action was to get rather too close for comfort on the evening of 1st October 1940, however, when a number of bombs were dropped on Okehampton itself during an isolated German raid. Miraculously, there were no serious injuries, despite of one of the bombs narrowly missing a cinema full of people. The local war effort included the Devon War Agriculture Committee's (DWAC) Transport Department, based at Barton Garage, which provided transport for members of the Women's Land Army and others to and from farms as well as offering driving instruction. Then, of course, there were several well-trained platoons of Home Guards in the district, like that made up of Meldon quarrymen. It was their job to protect industry and vital infrastructure such as the quarry and railway, as well as people and homes, in the event of the feared invasion.

Once again people from all walks of life rallied round enthusiastically to support the armed forces and do what they could to help the war effort. But the war also brought people together from very different backgrounds and inevitably caused tensions on occasions. There were American and Canadian troops preparing for D-Day at the Army Camp and a unit of the Polish Navy billeted at another camp above Oaklands (where the Rugby Club is now).

British troops included Army gunnery instructors from the Camp, RAF officers based at the Okehampton Aerodrome and local service personnel on home leave. In addition there were 'Land Girls' from all over the country – many based at Tenby House in Fairplace and children, evacuated from London and other cities to avoid the heavy bombing, staying with local families. Many farms also had charge of trustworthy Italian and German Prisoners of War who worked for them while other pisoners of war worked as mechanics for the DWAC. On at least one occasion such tensions led to a pitched battle in the streets as men, tense and highly-trained for battle in the run-up to D-Day, fought over the local girls or the honour of their country after a few beers at a dance. But there were to be no Military Police to break up the fighting when the real action was encountered across the Channel. Like their comrades in the Great War before them, tragically, many were never to return to their home countries and too many loved ones were to receive the dreaded telegram.

A 'Welcome Home Fund' was set up for those who were fortunate enough to return and, in 1945, the town and district celebrated the hard-won victory – first in Europe and then in the Far East. With food and other essentials in short supply for some time after the War, it was to be many years before things reached anything like normality again. Many had experienced a different way of life during those turbulent years and things would never be quite the same again. Sport and other social pursuits took on a new meaning as life was lived to the full. In time, electricity arrived in even the most remote districts along with labour-saving gadgets and the first televisions. Increasingly, the motor car became the principal mode of transport for many households and public transport services began to suffer cutbacks. More and more freight was transported by road and the A30 trunk road through the town became increasingly congested. In 1947, the Mayor of Okehampton, Walter Henry Passmore, proudly named the Southern Railway's 128-ton Westcountry class steam locomotive 'Okehampton'. But, within twenty five years, the regular passenger service to Exeter ceased and the station was closed. Freight traffic from Meldon Quarry continued however.

This marked a difficult period for the town, still with a population of little over 4,000. Despite continuing investment in the market site, competition and summer traffic congestion on the traditional Saturday market day, finally forced its closure when the auctioneers moved their operation to nearby Hatherleigh – thus bringing to an end over 900 years of history. A great deal of money was spent on renovating and extending the Town Hall complex, much of which was covered by the gift of Sydney Simmons for the building of a new

Town Hall. These developments culminated in 1973 with the opening of the Charter Hall to commemorate the granting of the 1623 Borough Charter by James I. However, in the local government reorganisation the following year, the town was to lose its ancient borough status also. In spite of the loss of many powers and privileges, the office of Mayor was kept up and the Town Council still plays an active role in local affairs.

Now, at the beginning of the twenty-first century, the town is experiencing a period of unprecedented growth. The second half of the twentieth century had seen increasing amounts of through traffic on the A30 trunk road and the town became a notorious bottleneck during the holiday season. The controversial Okehampton by-pass, cutting through the northern tip of Dartmoor National Park and the Courtenay's medieval deer park, was finally opened in 1988. The railway has recently been re-opened to passenger traffic during the summer months and a number of new industries have been attracted by the town's central position and good communications. The food processing industry is one of the largest employers, representing the town's ongoing links with the surrounding farming community. Regular farmers' markets are encouraging a return to the consumption of locally produced food such as that enjoyed when the market was operating. Other employment includes a growing tourism sector, retail and services. Okehampton still maintains a broad range of services, disproportionate to its size, due to its geographical position and large rural hinterland. Community life is as active as ever with numerous clubs and societies catering for a wide range of interests. Considerable public investment has also been made to help the district adjust to the loss of trade suffered after the opening the by-pass and, latterly, to help counter the effects of the foot and mouth crisis. Okehampton is at the centre of a number of walking and cycling routes, including the Tarka Trail, West Devon Way, Two Castles Trail and the National Cycle Route. These open up access to some of the finest landscapes in Devon, if not England.

But perhaps Okehampton's most precious treasure is a history stretching back some 2,000 years. Few places can claim to have such a broad range of historical subject matter, nor such a distinctive nature. It was for this reason that the Museum of Dartmoor Life was established in 1981, following an inaugural meeting, called by the late John Young, when he was President of the Rotary Club of Okehampton in 1976. The site was acquired in 1979 and consists of a fine set of nineteenth century buildings, including a three storey mill, an old printer's works and two cottages – one of which was the birthplace of Sydney Simmons. The picturesque cobbled courtyard, leading off West Street through a covered cart-way, is a rare survival of a once typical 'in-fill' yard within a medieval burgage plot. I had the privilege of being the first Curator of this museum, from 1981 to 1996. It offers a glimpse into the lives of the people of Dartmoor and the Okehampton district through the objects, photographs and documents they have left behind.

However, it is difficult to convey experiences, emotions and every day human relationships with objects alone and, whether you are an 'Oketonian' or not, I hope that this book has added a little to your understanding of the lives of some of the people who have contributed to the fascinating heritage we all share in old 'Ockington'.

NOTES

1. The area of modern Strasbourg
2. Only when the Spanish supplies ran short in the later centuries did the Roman Empire start to take an active interest in the Cornish tin industry by bringing it directly under Imperial control. There is no evidence to show that Dartmoor sources were exploited at this time but, equally, there is none to prove that they weren't.
3. The words mor coed appear in place names such as Morchard Bishop and Cruwys Morchard.
4. The small cattle were similar to the modern Dexter, the sheep like Soays and the pure-bred Dartmoor pony is thought to be a direct descendant of the horses that pulled British chariots into battle against the Roman legions.
5. As little stone was used in the construction of houses off the moor – timber and clay being in plentiful supply and easy to work with – there is little easily identifiable evidence for archaeologists to find. Consequently, it is very difficult to estimate how many houses and settlements existed.
6. Nemetostatio was one of a jumbled list of names appearing on a Roman itinerary known as the Ravenna Cosmography, a compilation of early road books published in the 7th century, which mapped out a route down the south-west peninsula. It has generally been associated with discoveries of various Roman sites around North Tawton because of the Nymet' name connection. 'Statio' probably refers to it being a tax collection point. Other places mentioned, including Tamaris (presumably at a crossing of the River Tamar), Uxella (meaning 'two rivers') and Devionissum Statio, have yet to be identified. Could Okehampton be among them?
7. This small fort was excavated in 1938, revealing stone faced banks flanking the entrance. It probably dates from the same period as the hill-forts which tower above the River Teign at Cranbrook, Wooston and Prestonbury – around 250 BC.
8. The site of this fort was discovered in the form of crop marks, identified in an aerial photograph taken during the dry summer of 1974. Subsequent trial excavations, consisting of cross-sections through the V-shaped ditch and rampart, uncovered various pieces of pottery from locally made to imported samian ware and fragments of the red clay roof tiles which once covered the timber and clay buildings within.
9. This is conjecture but a number of place names around North Tawton to the east – the probable Roman Nemetosatio – suggest a cult to Nemetona, the 'Goddess of the Sacred Grove' in the vicinity. Indeed, it is possible that the place referred to as Ochenemitona in the Domesday Book is a reference to the Castle site – from the elements oca, the 'sacred stream' of Nemetona – rather than the neighbouring Saxon settlement of Ocmundtune, the 'settlement by the Okement'. Archaeological evidence in the form of fragments of roof tiles of a probable Roman fabric and a carved stone head of distinctly Celtic style found in the in-fill of the ditch around the later Norman castle motte or mound, the distinctive natural features of the site and known practices elsewhere in Roman Britain and Gaul, all lend weight to the possibility).
10. Huna was one of those named as being freed by the Priest Brown on the Leofric Missal. Unfortunately, the name of his former master was obliterated and Osfers, the Saxon lord of Ocmundtune at the time of the Norman Conquest, has been assumed. However, Osfers held eleven manors in Devon and there is no indication as to where he actually lived. The rest of Huna's details are, of course, fictitious but based on general archaeological and documentary evidence from the period.
11. The notion of a lingering 'superstitious' meaning to a former pagan site here is conjecture but not unlikely. There are other examples of Norman mottes being built over former sacred sites

although this could be coincidental as they both tended to occupy prominent landscape features.
12. Apart from the early stone keep, no traces of any buildings – timber, clay or stone – from the initial phase have been found as they would probably have been obliterated by later developments It is not certain whether the motte and bailey were originally orientated this way. Remnants of a bank and ditch across the spur to the west may be evidence of an earlier arrangement or an additional defensive outwork. Alternatively, it could represent the site of the early borough referred to in the Domesday, or even a remnant of a pagan sacred enclosure. A cross-section, excavated in the early 1970s failed to find any firm dating evidence, although the construction was found to be similar to that of the motte and, therefore, probably contemporary with the earliest phase of the Norman castle.
13. This was the situation at Launceston where a market was established outside the castle walls, on the opposite side of the valley to the Saxon settlement and market of Llanstefan – the holy place of St. Stephen – and, eventually, became the centre of the town, taking away Llanstefan's status – hence the name Llanstefan's town or Launceston.
14. There is some debate as to whether this was the place referred to by this name in Hugh Courtenay's exchange agreement of 1292 but it seems more likely than not from the geographical description, despite the similarity with the name 'Brayhams' just north of the town.
15. Hawisia is a purely fictitious character but the description of her house and settlement are based on the archaeological evidence provided by excavations of one of the abandoned farmsteads in the Courtenay deer park by David Austin and his team between 1976 and 1978.
16. There is some doubt as to whether the inhabitants of the settlement were forcibly evicted or left of their own accord due to the deteriorating climate of the early 14th century as no records have survived.
17. Excavation suggests that earliest, all timber houses, were re-built in stone within the space of 100 years – probably by the succeeding generations of the same family. As the families grew, so houses were extended or new ones built nearby.
18. Produce for exchange or barter was still the main currency for most of the peasant class at this date and church tithes and manorial dues were also paid in kind.
19. Lady Eleanor and all of the Courtenays mentioned in the book are historical figures and the descriptions of the castle are based on architectural and archaeological records plus well-documented contemporary accounts of the lives and homes of medieval nobility.
20. Such private apartments would later become known as 'withdrawing' or, simply, 'drawing' rooms in time.
21. This list is actually based on the recorded 'familiars' or 'menie' of Earl Edward Courtenay in the 1380s. A menie was an extended group, bound to the lord by marriage or patronage. Damsels were unmarried ladies of rank.
22. It is assumed that the deer park was contemporary with the re-building of the castle. It must have been existence by 1306 when a piece of land was acquired from the lord of the sub-manor of Belstone for a deer leap.
23. These bells somehow found their way into the belfry of the small church of Tresmeer, just west of Launceston, possibly after the Reformation, and their place of origin became forgotten until an authority on church bells, Prebendary John Scott, recognised the rare, secular inscriptions in old English around their collars and dated them to the early 14th century. He suggested that the names matched those of Hugh and Eleanor Courtenay at the

right period and made the connection with Okehampton. The reference to catching game strongly suggests a link with the castle and deer park. At the time of writing, the bells have been loaned by the Parish to the Museum of Dartmoor Life so that they can be conserved and displayed near their original home.
24. Elizabeth Brock is another fictitious character although there was a Richard Brock recorded as holding the office of 'Provost' or Portreeve in 1296. Her life is based on various contemporary accounts of the lives of medieval women.
25. There are no records of any particular shops or businesses in Okehampton from this early and no direct architectural or archaeological evidence of the nature of the buildings. This description is really a best guess from the limited available evidence of towns in the South West at this period and later references to cob. The basic simple street layout and the burgage plots, which probably date from around this time, are still fossilised in the modern townscape and clearly visible on old maps however.
26. The ducking stool later kept just below the East Bridge although there is only one reference to it ever being used.
27. The area where George Street, St. James Street, Mill Road and Castle Road meet is known as Fairplace and may have been where pleasure fairs were held, away from the commercial centre of the town and just outside of the burgage plots stretching back from the southern side of Fore Street.
28. This earthwork can be found just on the higher side of the footpath, a few metres south west of Saxongate (Grid Ref. SX 582 932). It is marked on old Ordnance Survey maps as Chapel. The remnant of a door arch, lying on the ground along with part of a small, slit window may have led antiquarians to believe the building was a religious building but there is no record of such a structure in the vicinity. It has also been associated with a leper hospital. Such buildings often had narrow slits for passing food through to the unfortunate sufferers within. However, recent examination of the hillside has revealed a track leading from the castle to near this spot and it seems a likely candidate for a lodge, which must have existed somewhere in the vicinity.
29. From the term 'bubo' – the characteristic swelling of the lymphatic gland.
30. There were originally two houses built against the chapel walls, Mount Ribbon and Jane's House are recorded from the 16th century and a third, Treween's House, was added some time in the 18th century and belonged to the parish. It was later divided into two.
31. These were excavated prior to the Okehampton by-pass construction and showed the typical tinners' method of successive diversions of the river in order to dig the alluvial materials and 'wash' the gravel so as to separate-out the heavier cassiterite (tin) particles as they worked up the valley.
32. There are the remains of a tinner's mill on the right bank of the Taw (Grid ref. SX 621 921) and very scanty remains of a mill near Watersglide on the East Okement (Grid ref. 597 940).
33. The passages in italics are, as far as possible, accurate extracts from the journals of John Rattenbury, Town Clerk 1624 – 1655. These were later copied by Richard Shebbeare and are now in the Devon Record Office. Various writers have attempted to transcribe the journals down the years but the original Rattenbury journals and some pages from Shebbeare's copy are missing so we have to trust the accuracy later transcripts for some parts.
34. The person responsible for receiving property forfeited to the Crown if its owner died intestate and without heirs.
35. This list of possessions is based on the probate inventory of Francis Rattenbury of

Okehampton who died in 1673 and reflects the limited number of possessions held even by the wealthier inhabitants of Okehampton at this time.
36. The word curfew comes from the French 'couvrefeu' – cover fire.
37. The process of cleansing and thickening newly woven cloth. It was first soaked in stale cattle urine to dissolve the 'yoke' or natural grease of the sheep's wool and then passed under fulling stocks – heavy wooden mallets, lifted by cams on a water-powered shaft, in a soapy mixture of fuller's earth. This felted the fibres together thus giving it a 'fuller' appearance and making it stronger and warmer. It was then washed with clean water and stretched out to dry on racks between rows of 'tenter hooks' (the origin of the term for being kept in suspense) to prevent it from shrinking. It was then dyed (if not done at the spinning stage) and the nap raised with teazles before being trimmed to size with shears and pressed. Fulling mills were also called 'tucking' mills in Devon after the process of tucking the cloth under the fulling stocks – hence the surname Tucker.
38. Among other sums, Richard Harragroe left £50 in order to provide an annual income of £5 for a 'learned and painful schoolmaster', which, along with the contribution of the mayor and corporation, enabled six or eight poor children could be 'brought up in the fear of God and good letters for ever'.
39. This was probably the small, square enclosure with a double ditch and bank, which is thought to have been the Roman signal station mentioned in Chapter 1. A section through the defences, excavated prior to the construction of the new A30 dual carriageway across Sourton Down, failed to find any dateable evidence. The same excavations also uncovered an unexpected medieval 'long house' and uncovered a section of an ancient metalled track way, suspected of being Roman but, again, failing to give up any dating evidence other than the fact that it was still being used when the long house was occupied.
40. This bridge used to stand near Bear Farm, just below the confluence of the two rivers on the old Jacobstowe road. Knowle Bridge replaced it when the road was diverted by the Turnpike Trust in 1820.
41. This subsequently became known as Market Street as the market developed and became centred in this area.
42. By this date, most mining was conducted via shallow, vertical shafts or horizontal 'adits' driven into the hillside but, apart from alluvial tin, most of the areas mineral wealth remained undiscovered or commercially exploited.
43. Sabine Baring-Gould recorded this story, from the recollections of an elderly parishioner of Lewtrenchard in the latter half of the 19th century.
44. At the time of writing parts of this building survive in the Castle Hospital complex, including the entrance nearest to the river.
45. This building still stands at the junction of New Road and High Street having been superceded with the building of the new Weslyan Methodist church at Fairplace in 1904. After that, the old chapel was variously used as a garage (Days), ice rink and an outdoor activities shop before coming back into religious use as a New Life Centre.
46. This chapter is built around the life of Dora Weekes, from her own reminiscences and those of her sister, Floss, plus general information on the town at that time gleaned from oral history recordings, newspaper cuttings etc.
47. A large photograph of Private Ward wearing the numerous medals he won for shooting, and some of the medals themselves, are on display in the Museum of Dartmoor Life.
48. Iam grateful to Fred Barlow of Northfield Road for this recollection.
49. This ceremony now takes place every five years but, sadly, minus the spurling!

50. The castle was passed to the safekeeping of the Ministry of Public Buildings and Works in 1967 and is now in the care of English Heritage.
51. A cell window from this Police Station was set into the river bank on the higher side of the old West Bridge by Eustace Worden, who lived on the site of the old town jail there. It can be seen in some old photographs of the bridge and has given rise to the common misinterpretation that it was actually a remnant of the old jail. in fact, its cell windows faced the street, not the river.

BIBLIOGRAPHY

Austin, D., *Excavations in Okehampton Deer Park, Devon 1976-1978*. Devon Archaeological Society Proceedings No. 36, 1978.
Austin, D., Daggett, R. H. And Walker, M. J. C. *Farms and Fields in Okehampton Park, Devon: the Problems of Studying Medieval Landscape.* Landscape History 2, 1980.
Balkwill, C. J. *A Roman Site at Okehampton.* Proceedings of the Devon Archaeological Society No. 34, 1976.
Baring-Gould, Sabine. *A Book of Folklore.* Methuen & Co, 1913 (reprinted by Praxis Books, 1993).
Barrow, R. H. *The Romans.* Penguin Books Ltd, Harmondsworth, 1949 (reprinted 1977).
Bidwell, P. T., Bridgewater, R. And Silvester, R. J. *The Roman Fort at Okehampton, Devon.* Britannia 10, 1979.
Burke, John. *History of England.* Collins, London, 1974.
Butler, Jeremy. *Dartmoor Atlas of Antiquities. Volume Two – The North.* Devon Books, Exeter, 1991.
Coxhead, J. R. W. *Legends of Devon.* Western Press, 1954.
Davison, Michael Worth (Ed). *Everyday Life Through the Ages.* The Reader's Digest Association Ltd., London, 1992.
Eluere, Christiane, *The Celts. First Masters of Europe.* Thames and Hudson Ltd., London, 1993.
Eyles, Sarah and Wheeleker, Susannah. *Poor Relief in Devon.* The Devonshire Association, Exeter, 1991.
Falkus, Malcolm and Gillingham, John. *Historical Atlas of Britain.* Book Club Associates, London, 1981.
Finberg, H. P. R. *The House of Orfgar and the Foundation of Tavistock Abbey.* April 1943.
Fleming, Andrew. *The Dartmoor Reaves. Investigating Prehistoric Land Divisions.* B. T. Batsford Ltd, London, 1988.
Fox, Aileen. *South West England 3,500 BC - AD 600.* David & Charles, Newton Abbot, 1973.
Geen, M. S. *An Ordinary Devon Family. Geen of Okehampton.* Private Publication, 1975.
Haslam, Jeremy. *Early Medieval Towns in Britain.* Shire Publications Ltd, Princes Risborough, 1985.
Hemery, Eric. *High Dartmoor. Land and People.* Robert Hale, London, 1983.
Higham, R. A. *Okehampton Castle, Devon.* English Heritage, London, 1984.
Higham, R. A. *Excavations at Okehampton Castle, Devon. Part 1: The Motte and Keep.* Reprinted from Devon Archaeolical Proceedings No. 35, 1977.
Higham, R. A. and Allan, J. P. *Excavations at Okehampton Castle, Devon. Part 2: The Bailey. A Preliminary Report.* Devon Archaeological Society Proceedings No. 38, 1980.
Hindle, Brian Paul. *Medieval Town Plans.* Shire Publications Ltd., Princes Risborough, 1990.
Hoskins, W. G., *Devon.* Collins, London, 1954.
Hutton, Ronald. *The Stations of the Sun. A History of the Ritual Year in Britain.* Oxford University Press, Oxford, 1996.
Hall, Jean. *Railway Landmarks in Devon.* David & Charles, Newton Abbot, 1982.
Le Messurier, Brian (Ed.). *Crossing's Dartmoor Worker.* David & Charles, Newton Abbot, 1966.

Loudon, J. C. *An Encyclopaedia of Cottage, Farm and Villa Architecture and Furniture.* Longman, Brown, Green and Longmans, London, 1846.
Martin, E. W. *The Shearers and the Shorn.* Routledge & Kegan Paul Ltd, London, 1975.
Morris, John. *The Age of Arthur. A History of the British Isles from 350 to 650.* The History Book Club, London, 1973.
Muir, Richard. *Shell Guide to Reading the Landscape.* Michael Joseph Ltd, London, 1981.
Peachey, Stuart. *The Battles of Launceston and Sourton Down 1643.* Stuart Press, Bristol, 1993.
Pettit, Paul. *Prehistoric Dartmoor.* David & Charles, Newton Abbot, 1974.
Pevsner, Niklaus. *The Buildings of Devon.* Penguin Books, London, 1989.
Planel, Philippe. *Okehampton Castle. A Handbook for Teachers.* English Heritage, 1992.
Richards, Julian. *Meet the Ancestors. Unearthing the Evidence that Brings us Face to Face with the Past.* BBC Wordwide Ltd, 1999.
Roberts, Brian K. *Village Plans.* Shire Publications Ltd., Princes Risborough, 1982.
Ross, Anne. *Pagan Celtic Britain.* Constable & Co. Ltd., London, 1992.
Staines, Robin. *A History of Devon.* Philimore & Co. Ltd., Chichester, 1986.
Starkey, F. H. *Dartmoor Crosses.* A. Wheaton & Co., Exeter, 1989.
Taverner, R. L. *The History of the Churches of Okehampton with Inwardleigh.* The British Publishing Co. Ltd., Gloucester, c. 1969.
Various. *Archaeology of the Devon Landscape. Over 5000 Years of Devon's Heritage.* County Planning Department, Devon County Council, 1980.
Various. *Devon's Traditional Buildings.* County Amenities and Countryside Committee, Devon County Council, c. 1978?
Williams, Michael. *Curiosities of Devon.* Bossiney Books, Bodmin, 1983.
Wood, Margaret. *The English Mediaeval House.* Ferndale Editions, London.
Worth, R. H. *Worth's Dartmoor.* David & Charles, Newton Abbot, 1967.
Wreford, H & M. *Okehampton Collection*, Vollumes I - III.
Wright, W. H. K. *Some Account of the Baronry and Town of Okehampton: Its Antiquities and Institutions.* William Masland, Tiverton, 1889.
Young, Edward H. *Parochial Histories of Devonshire No. 1. Okehampton.* The Devonshire Association for the Advancement of Science, Literature and Art, Exeter, 1931.
Ziegler, Philip. *The Black Death.* The History Book Club, London, 1969.

Miscellaneous Papers:

Brailsford, J. W. *Excavations at the Promontory Fort near Okehampton Station.* Devon Archaeological Exploration Society, c. 1940.
Kerr, J. B. *Archaeology and the A30 Okehampton Bypass. Rescue Excavations in 1986 in Advance of Road Construction.* Summary Report, English Heritage Central Excavation Unit, 1987.
Maxfield, V. A. *Soldier and Civilian: Life Beyond the Ramparts.* 8th Caerleon Lecture, National Museum of Wales.
Sale Catalogue. *The Oaklands Estate, Okehampton, Devonshire.* Messrs. Driver, Surveyors, Land Agents & Auctioneers, London, 1877 (Museum of Dartmoor Life archive).
Taverner, R. L. *(Okehampton) The Seventeenth Century.* Unpublished private research notes, 2000 (Museum of Dartmoor Life archive).

Thomas, A. C. *And Shall These Mute Stones Speak?*, 1994.

Unknown. *Rise and Fade – Cymbeline.* Newspaper Cutting, 1881 (source unknown – Museum of Dartmoor Life archive).

Unknown. *Daring Burglary. Jewellers Shop Rifled at Okehampton, the Thieves Captured.* Newspaper Cutting, September 24, 1906 (source unknown –Museum of Dartmoor Life archive).

Unknown. *Mr. Sydney Simmons Honoured at Okehampton Last Night. Complimentary Banquet.* Newspaper Cutting, Friday September 11, 1908 (source unknown – Museum of Dartmoor Life archive).

Unknown. *King Carnival. Okehampton's Magnificent First Effort a Big Success.* Newspaper Cutting, Thursday December 9, 1909 (source unknown – Museum of Dartmoor Life archive).

Unknown. *Lydford Saxon Town and Castle.* Department of the Environment Guide, HMSO, 1982.

Warren, F. E. (Ed). *The Leofric Missal*, 1883.

INDEX

Adeliza, daughter of Baldwin 20
Aerodrome, Folly Gate 118-119
Aethelston, King 11
Agricultural Show 111
Albermarle, Duke of 66
Alfred the Great, King 11
All Saints, Parish Church of 10, 11, 19, 20, 35, 42, 89, 91, 117
Almshouses, Simmons 117
America 83, 90, 109, 110
American troops 119
Anglican Church 82
Arcade, The 97, 116
Army 96, 102, 119
Arscott, Edmund 59
Arthur, King 10
Arthur, King 10
Arundel family 45
Arundel, Earl of 44
Ashburton 43
Ashbury 81
Atkinson, Christopher 76
Augustan, Second Legion 1, 8
Augustine, Saint 11
Australia 90
Austyn, Thomas 65

Back Street 52-53
Baldwin de Brionne 15, 17, 19-20, 27
Baldwin, Monk of Forde Abbey 20
Bands 93, 96, 108, 110
Baring, Sir Thomas 78
Baring-Gould, Rev. Sabine 48, 126
Barlow, Fred 126
Barnstaple 11, 76
Barton Garage 119
Barton Road 81
Beare Bridge 70
Beare Farm 126
Bec Abbey, Normandy 19
Bedford, Duke of 46
Beer, Sgt. 104
Beeting of the Bounds 110
Belstone 39, 89, 124
Benedictine Order 20, 22
Bible Christian Church 82
Bickle, Captain 56
Bideford 81, 87
Bidwell, Thomas 59
Bindon, Battle of 10
Black Death, the 40-41
Black-a-ven Brook 43
Blackdown Copper Mine 93
Blackford, William 63
Blatchford, builder 97
Blitz, the 119
Boer War 107
Bohun, Margaret de 39

Bonville, Lord 44
Borough Lands 47
Borough of Okehampton 23, 35, 37, 45, 47, 50, 51, 55-64, 72-3, 77, 93, 98, 103, 121
Bower, Richard 65
Bowling Green 65, 117
Brackentor Reservoir 98
Brayhams 124
Bremelcombe, John 63
Bremelcombe, Mr. 59
Bridestowe 9, 60, 66, 81, 88-89, 116
Bridges 35, 41, 47, 70, 81, 91-94, 96-97, 116-117, 125-127
Bridget, Saint 9
Brightley 19
Brittany 10
Broadbury 6
Broadmoor Lane 18
Broadwoodwidger 40
Brock, Grace 66
Brock, Richard 35, 66, 125
Brock, Robert 57
Bronscombe, Bishop 10, 20
Bronze Age 2, 23
Brown, Priest 13
Buck, John & Nathaniel 69, 73
Bude Canal 81
Bude 96
Buller family 45
Burgage plots 51, 90, 122, 125
Burgoine, Squire 70
By-pass 118, 121, 125
Byrham 23-27, 32, 34, 39

Calmady, Josias 66
Calmady, Sir Shilstone 59
Calmady-Hamlyn, Squire 81
Can, Edmund, the Elder 57
Can, Peter 65
Canadian troops 119
Canal, Bude 81
Canute, King 12
Carnival 110
Cary, Sir George 70
Castle Chapel 20, 30
Castle Hospital 117, 126
Castle Lane/Road 66, 88, 125
Castle, Okehampton 16-17, 19, 23, 27-33, 40, 44-45, 49, 73, 78-79, 93, 117, 123-125, 127
Catholic, Roman 41, 46, 53, 61, 70
Celts/Celtic 1-2, 7, 9-10, 12, 16
Centwine, King 10
Chagford 43
Chapel, St. James 20, 30, 35, 37, 47, 52, 55, 67, 72, 91, 98, 103, 113, 117-118

Chapel, St. John's, Market Street 98
Charities 66-67, 71, 87, 98, 117
Charles I, King 54, 58, 61
Charles II, King 66, 70
Charter Hall 98, 122
Charters 19, 47, 70, 98, 121
Chatham, Earl of 72
Chichacott 17-18
Chivalry, code of 31
Choir Boys' Path 74
Christians - early 8-9
Chudleigh, Major James 60-61
Church Lane 40
Church Wardens 42-43, 47, 77
Church, All Saints 11, 19, 20, 35, 42, 70, 89, 91, 117
Cinemas 106, 113-114, 119
Cistercian Order 19-20
Civil War, The 49, 59-62, 71
Clannaborough Farm, Throwleigh 113
Clapps Mill 95, 116
Clerk, Town 47, 50, 64-5, 69, 125
Climate 2, 19, 23, 116
Clive, Lord, of India 72
Cloth industry (see also wool) 43, 83, 126
Cobham, Sir Alan 119
Combe, barber & bandmaster 111
Common land 3, 12, 43, 80, 89, 114
Commonwealth, The 65
Conservative Club 114
Cornish Army, The 60
Cornish's, Jewellers 104
Cornovii 5
Cornwall 46, 50, 57, 60, 93
Corporation (see also Town Council) 47, 52, 53-64, 70, 72, 78-80, 98, 115, 126
Cottle, George 57
Courtenay, Agnes 27-33, 38
Courtenay, Dame Joan 42
Courtenay, Edward, 10th Earl of Devon 45
Courtenay, Edward, 3rd Earl of Devon 45, 124
Courtenay, Edward, 7th Earl of Devon 44-45
Courtenay, Gertrude of Landrake 49
Courtenay, Hawisia 20
Courtenay, Henry, 9th Earl of Devon 45
Courtenay, Hugh I 27, 124
Courtenay, Hugh II, 1st Earl of Devon 27-33, 35, 37
Courtenay, Hugh III, 2nd Earl of Devon 39
Courtenay, Hugh of Hacombe & Boconoc 45

131

Courtenay, John, son of 6th Earl of Devon	44	
Courtenay, Katherine	45	
Courtenay, Lady Eleanor	27-33, 38-39, 124	
Courtenay, Margaret	44	
Courtenay, Reginald	20	
Courtenay, Robert	19, 21, 35	
Courtenay, Thomas, 5th Earl of Devon	44	
Courtenay, Thomas, 6th Earl of Devon	44	
Courtenay, William, 8th Earl of Devon	45	
Courtenay, William, Archbishop	39	
Courts – law	15, 35, 43, 47-48, 70	
Cowick Priory	20, 39, 42	
Cranmere Pool	67	
Crawford, Matthew	89	
Crediton	10, 11, 46, 104	
Crime	35, 47, 57, 103	
Crocker, George	56	
Crosses	9, 34, 47, 51, 70	
Cryer	20, 35, 37	
Curfew Bell	52, 90, 103, 106, 113, 126	
Customs	42, 55, 65, 84, 110, 112	
Danes	11-13	
Darcy, Thomas	49	
Darkey Lane	19	
Dartmoor National Park	121	
Day, Thomas & Sons	94, 105, 116, 126	
Deer Park, Castle	24, 30, 39-40, 45, 121, 124-125	
Denvorn, Robert de	20	
Devon Copper Mine	94	
Devon Motor Transport Co.	116	
Devon War Agricultural Committee	119-120	
Devonshire Regiment	103, 114	
Dissolution of the Monasteries	45, 53	
Domesday Survey	11, 17-18, 41, 124	
Drew, Christopher	63	
Drew, William	57, 63	
Drill Hall	65, 114	
Duchy of Cornwall	96	
Ducking Stool	35, 47, 52, 125	
Dumnonia	1-2, 8-10	
Dunn, Sir William	109	
Durotriges	1	
Dyrham, Battle of	10	
East Bridge	52, 92, 94, 96-97, 125	
East Hill	76, 108	
East Okement Farm	43	
East Okement River	43, 93, 96	
East Street	94, 117	
Economy	47	
Education	54, 67, 83, 87-88
Edward I, King	23, 27, 35, 39
Edward II, King	39
Edward III, King	39
Edward IV, King	44-46
Egbert, King	10
Electricity generating plant	97
Ellacott, John	69
Ellis, Agar	86
Employment	44, 71, 81-82, 85, 90, 93, 95, 121
Enclosures	89
Endacott, William, Thomas and Louie	113
English Heritage	127
Essex, Earl of	61-62
Exeter Cathedral	39, 44
Exeter Road	117
Exeter	1, 5, 8, 11-2, 15, 17-18, 20, 37, 46, 54, 57, 72, 96, 104, 110, 113, 119
Exeter, Marquis of	45
Ezard, Billy	113
Factories	82, 94-95, 103, 114-116
Fairfax, Sir Thomas	62
Fairplace	74, 101, 120, 125-126
Fairs	37, 67, 84-85, 111
Fatherford Viaduct	43
Fenny Bridges, Battle of	46
Feudal System	17, 22-24, 27, 35, 41, 78
Finch Foundry, Sticklepath	94
Finch, William	94
Finney, Thomas	63
Fires/Fire Brigade	103, 111, 115
First World War	99, 113-115, 120
Fitz John, John	36
Fitz, Mary	49
Fitz, Sir John	49
Fitzford House, Tavistock	48-49
Folly Gate	118
Forde Abbey	20, 30
Fore Street	19, 37, 50-51, 96-97, 102, 111, 125
Forest Mine	93
Forest of Dartmoor	32, 35, 37, 40
Forts, Romans	5-8
Fosse Way	5
France/French	15, 17, 35, 41, 46, 61, 73-75
Fyner, Thomas	65
Gafolforda	11
Galford	11
Gas Company	96
Gaul	1, 7
Gayer, Benjamin	67-68
Geen, Charles	94, 97
Geen, Henry	97
George Street	41, 117, 125
George V, King	118
German, W.B., boot factory	95, 116
Germany/German	46, 119, 120
Gidley, Justice	70
Giglet Fair	84, 112
Gilbert, Count of Brionne	15
Glanville, John	54
Glass Factory, Meldon	115
Glass, James, Foundry	94
Gliddon, Thomas, tailor	74
Godwin, Earl of Wessex	15
Grammar School	47, 52, 55, 65, 67, 83, 87
Granulite Quarry, Meldon	94, 115
Great War, The	99, 113-115, 120
Great Western Railway	96
Grenville, Sir Richard	49, 62
Guiger, son of Baldwin	19
Guildhall (see also Town Hall)	47, 52, 53, 70, 78, 81
Gunn's Mineral Water Works	94
Halstock	93, 96
Hare, John	36
Harold I, King of Wessex	13, 15, 17
Harragroe, Richard	54, 66, 126
Harry, Seth, grocers	97
Harter Farm	43
Hastings, Battle of	13
Hatherleigh	120
Heaynes, Mr	59
Hellyons, William	46
Henrietta Maria, Queen	61
Henry VI, King	44
Henry VIII, King	45
High Street	19, 40, 80, 91, 117, 126
Hillforts	1, 6, 10, 123
Hockin, Rev. John	72
Holley, James Hunt	87, 93
Holley, Major General	98, 103, 109, 114
Holsworthy	81, 96
Holy Wells	40-41
Home Guard, The	119
Hook Wood	35
Hopkins, Roger, engineer	81
Hopton, Sir Ralph	60
Horwell, Mr.	111
Hospitals	117, 125, 126
Housing	87, 96
Howard, Charles	49
Howard, Lady Francis	49
Howard, Lady Mary	48
Huna	13-16
Hussey, Rev. John	66
Ice Works, Sourton	89
Industry	43, 71, 77, 83, 89, 92, 95, 121

Inns	52, 84, 92, 97	
Inwardleigh		47
Ireland/Irish		9, 89, 93
Iron Age		3, 8, 12
Isca (Roman Exeter)		1, 8
Italy/Italian		46, 120
Jacobstowe		126
James I, King	47, 49, 54, 122	
James II, King		70
James, Saint		20-21
James, Saint, Chapel of	20, 30, 35, 37, 42, 47, 52, 55, 67, 72, 91, 98, 103, 113, 117-118	
Jane's House		125
Justice	15, 35-36, 47-48, 54, 77, 82	
Jutes		9
Kelly, Joane		63
Kelly, John		63
Kempley Road		94
Kigbeare	17-18, 42, 47, 66	
King Way		48, 89
Kingsley, Charles		90
Knowle Bridge		126
Landrake		49
Latin	8-9, 30, 46-47, 53	
Launceston	19, 22, 60, 124	
Leawood, Bridestowe		66
Leofric, Bishop		11
Leper Hospital		125
Letcher, Randall		35
Lethbridge		46
Lewdown		107
Lewtrenchard		11, 48, 126
Lifton		11, 61
Liwtune (Lifton)		11
Lodge Bridge		93, 96, 115
Lodge Road		78, 80, 94
London	39, 66, 71-72, 76, 84, 86, 97, 100-101, 105, 108-109, 112, 120	
Loyal Okehampton Infantry Regiment		75
Lydford	11-13, 18, 22, 43, 96	
Lyndhurst, Lord Chancellor		86
Maddaford Farm		47
Maggies Lane		18
Magistrates		105
Mail, Royal		84
Manor of Okehampton		80
Mansion Court, East Street		117
Market Hall	103, 112-113, 115	
Market Street	94, 98, 126	
Market	17-18, 20, 22, 33-35, 45, 47-48, 51, 67, 81, 84, 98, 111-112, 115, 120-121	
Marvin, Richard		63

Mary, Queen		45
Mary, Saint, Chapel of		20
Maurice, Prince		61
May pole		59
Mayor	47, 54-64, 67, 69, 77, 114, 121, 126	
Mayville, Fairplace		101
Meldon Quarry		94, 120
Meldon Reservoir		93
Meldon Viaduct		94
Meldon	60, 81, 93-94, 96, 115, 119, 120	
Memorial stones		8
Metal working		3, 5
Methodist Church	83, 91, 94, 126	
Meules, France		17
Middle Row	52, 78, 81, 90-91, 96, 117	
Military Sidings		96, 102
Mill Road		65, 95, 125
Millet, Pierre		74
Mills	17, 25, 35, 43-44, 69, 71, 95, 103, 116, 125	
Mines	83, 92-94, 126	
Mint		13
Miracle Plays		42
Mohun		45
Mohun, Lord John	56, 58-59	
Mollis, Roger de		17
Moretonhampstead		71
Mount Ribbon		125
Museum of Dartmoor Life	74, 108, 115, 121, 126	
Napoleonic Wars		73-75
Navy, Royal		57
Nemetostatio		5
New Model Army		62
New Road		19
New Road	80, 94, 105, 126	
Newcombe, Fire Brigade Captain		111
Newcombe, Simon		104-105
Newecum, John, Vicar		42
Newton Abbot		107
Non-conformist churches		82
Norleigh, Squire Henry		66
Normandy		15, 17, 19
Normans	12-13, 15-17, 79, 123	
North Lane/Road/Street	81, 88	
North Tawton		71, 123
Northampton, Battle of		44
Northfield Road		126
Northmore House		69, 78
Northmore, John		69
O'Bryan, William		82
Oake, Roger		57
Oaklands Mansion	76-87, 91, 98-99, 109, 118-119	
Ocmundtune	12-17, 19, 123	

Okehampton Artillery Camp	96, 102-3, 118-119	
Okehampton Brick Company		116
Okehampton By-pass	118-119, 120	
Okehampton Gas Company		96
Okehampton Hamlets Parish	88, 110	
Okehampton Mine		93
Okehampton Railway Station	96, 120	
Okehampton Union		88
Okehampton Wheal Friendship Mine		94
Okement River	6, 11, 16, 101	
Okement, East, River	43, 93, 96	
Okement, West, River	7, 43-44, 93-94, 117	
Osfers, Saxon Thane	13, 17, 123	
Ottery, River		10
Pagan		1, 7, 9
Paltridge, builder		97
Pankhurst, Emilie		102
Pannage, right of		12, 27, 37
Pannier Market		98, 111
Parade, The		50, 52
Parish Church of All Saints	10-11, 19, 20, 35, 42, 70, 89, 91, 117	
Parker, Lewes		66
Parker, Mr.		59
Parklands		113
Parliament	35, 55, 57, 58-60, 62, 66, 70-72, 77, 80, 85, 99	
Parliamentary Reform		87
Passmore, Walter Henry		120
Penselwood, Battle of		10
Percy, Sir Alan		49
Petrock, Saint		9
Petrockstowe		9
Picture Houses	106, 113-114, 119	
Picture Palace Cinema		114
Pilton, Barnstaple		11
Pitt, Thomas, MP		72
Pitt, William, the Elder, MP		72
Plague		41, 54, 67
Plymouth	59, 74, 96, 104, 109, 119	
Plympton		43
Polard, Sir Amos		70
Pole, Cardinal		45
Police Station	91, 104, 117, 127	
Polish Navy		119
Politics	79, 98, 108	
Poor Law/rates/relief	66, 70-71, 82, 85, 87	
Population	11, 18, 23, 34-35, 41, 66, 73, 82, 85, 98, 120	
Porter, Michael		57
Portreeve/Provost	20, 23, 35, 37, 47, 125	
Posbury, Battle of		10
Posentesbyrig, Battle of		10
Post Office		106

Pounds	52, 57	
Powderham Castle	39	
Prayer Book Rebellion	46	
Premier Cinema	114	
Presbyterian Church	66, 70	
Princetown	74, 89	
Principius	9	
Priory (Brightley)	19	
Prisons	35, 43, 52, 54, 74, 91, 127	
Prisoners of War	73-75, 120	
Protestant	53, 59, 67	
Punishment	15, 35, 48, 54, 101	
Puritan	50, 53, 65-66	
Pye, Sir Robert	61	
Quakers	70, 82	
Quarries	81, 83, 93, 94, 115-116, 120	
Railways	8, 81, 84, 87, 95-6, 98, 120-121	
Rainer, Castle Steward	17	
Ramsley Copper Mine, South Zeal	93	
Ranelagh Road	19	
Rattenbury, Francis	125	
Rattenbury, John	50-65, 69, 125	
Rattenbury, Peter	50	
Rattlebrook Peat Works	116	
Reading Room	88	
Reaves	3	
Recorder, Borough	47	
Red-a-ven Brook	43	
Reddaway, Edward	70	
Reddaway, Thomas	57	
Redvers, de, family	27-28	
Reformation, The	20, 41, 124	
Richard, son of Baldwin	19	
Roads	2, 5-6, 8, 19, 40, 42, 44, 47, 71, 81-84, 87, 89, 117-118, 120-121	
Robert, son of Baldwin	19	
Roberts, L	61	
Roche, Saint	41	
Rock Well	41	
Rome/Roman	1, 2, 5, 7-9, 11, 123, 126	
Rooles, Dennis, Sheriff	58	
Rosemary Row	117	
Roses, Wars of the	44	
Royal Air Force	118-120	
Royal Mail	84	
Royal Navy	57	
Royalist Army	60	
Rugby Club	119	
Russell, Lord	46	
Sacred Sites	2	
Sampford Courtenay	20, 46, 104	
Sanitation	34, 87, 96, 113	
Savile, Albany Bourchier	77, 87	
Savile, Bourchier Wrey, Rev.	77, 87, 91	
Savile, Christopher	76	
Savile, Jane	76	
Savile, Squire Albany	76-86, 87, 91, 98, 115	
Saxongate	125	
Saxons	8-13, 15, 17, 19	
Schools	47, 52, 55, 65, 67, 83, 87-88, 92, 101	
Scotland	35, 58, 75, 89	
Second World War	117-118, 120	
Seth Harry's Grocery Store	97	
Settlement, Laws of	70, 88	
Seymour, Edward, ('Protector' Somerset)	46	
Seymour, Lord	86	
Shambles, The	51, 53, 69, 81	
Sharp Hill	19, 80	
Shebbear	82	
Shebbeare, John	63	
Shebbeare, Richard	64-65, 70, 125	
Sherbourne, See of	12	
Shob Hill	19, 80	
Simmon's Park	108-109	
Simmons, Sydney	88, 108-109, 111, 117, 120-121	
Simmons, Thomas	88	
Slade, William	57	
Slaves	1, 10, 11, 13, 19	
Smale, Mr.	111	
Smiths, metal	5, 13, 44, 92	
Somerset, Earl of	44	
Sourton Down	6, 9, 60, 126	
Sourton	88, 89	
Southern Railway	120	
Spain	1	
Spanish Armada	57	
Sport and Leisure	120	
Sprague, Joseph	65	
Spurling, custom of	55, 110, 126	
St. George	41	
St. James Chapel	20, 30, 35, 37, 42, 47, 52, 55, 67, 72, 91, 98, 103, 113, 117, 118	
St. James Street	125	
St. James, Feast of	21, 27, 33, 37	
St. John's Chapel, Market Street	98	
St. Mary's Chapel, Brightley	20	
St. Roche	40	
Staffordshire	115	
Stannaries (see also tin)	35, 42-43	
Station Road	103	
Station, Okehampton	96, 120	
Sticklepath	82	
Stocks	35, 48	
Stone Age	2	
Stoney Park Lane	19	
Stoney Park	60	
Stowford	9	
Stratton, Battle of	61	
Suffolk, Earl of	49	
Sunday School	83, 91, 101, 106-107	
Sweetlands	78	
Tamar, River	5, 10, 12	
Tavistock Abbey	12, 22, 39, 45-46	
Tavistock	22, 43, 48, 71, 89, 96, 101	
Taw, River	44	
Tawstock, Barnstaple	76	
Taxes/tithes	43, 55	
Tedburn St. Mary	40	
Temperance Hotel	101	
Tenby House, Fairplace	120	
Tewkesbury, Battle of	44	
Thomas, Edward	58-59	
Throwleigh,	113	
Tin	1, 35, 42-44, 83, 123, 125-126	
Tintagel	9	
Tithe Map	91	
Tithes	27, 42, 124	
Tiverton Castle	27-28	
Toll Houses	81	
Tolls	35, 37	
Tories	86	
Totnes	11	
Tourism	95, 122	
Tower of London	45, 49, 58	
Town Clerk	47, 50, 64-65, 69, 125	
Town Council (see also Corporation & Borough)	121	
Town Hall (see also Guildhall)	47, 70, 78, 105, 120-121, 125	
Town Lands	47	
Town Mills	95	
Townsend, 'Turnip'	89	
Towton, Battle of	44	
Trade Unions	82	
Trade	2, 5, 8, 19, 40, 43-44, 47, 52, 71, 77, 82-83, 92, 111, 121	
Transport (see also Roads & Railways)	72, 81-83, 120	
Trelawny	45	
Treloar, Sir William	108-109	
Trethurffe family	45	
Treween's House	125	
Turner, J.M., Artist	73	
Turnpike Trust	19, 71, 77, 80, 82, 84, 91, 126	
Turpin, William	63	
Tyrwhit, Thomas	89	
Underhill	46	
Vagabonds	71	
Vespasianus, General Titus Flavius	1	
Vicarage	107	
Victoria, Queen	91, 108	
Vincent, Gilles	73	
Vivian family	45	

Vokins, Charles, architect	79, 91	
Wakefield, Battle of	44	
Wales, Prince of	105, 119	
Wales/Welsh	8-9, 19, 35, 65, 93	
Wallabrook	10	
War Memorial Hospital	117	
War Office	96	
Ward, Private William Thomas	103, 126	
Wars of the Roses	44	
Waverley Abbey, Surrey	19	
Weekes, Dora Emilie	100-113, 126	
Weekes, Tom, Flora Jane, William, Ada Jane, Flora and Elsie	100-113	
Weeks, Johane	58	
Weeks, William	58	
Welfare	71, 106, 114, 117	
Welles, Thomas	65	
Wellington, Duke of	86	
Wesley, John and Charles	82	
Wessex	10-11, 15	
West Bridge	41, 52, 91, 93, 116-117, 127	
West of England Compressed Peat Co,	116	
West Okement, River	7, 43, 93-94, 117	
West Quay	52	
West Street	74, 109, 116-117	
Westacott Farm	47	
Westcott, T.C., Drapers	100	
Westminster	76-77	
Westward Ho!	90	
Whigs	85-86	
White Hart Hotel	99, 108-109	
Whittacker, Laurence	58-59	
Wigney	93	
William, Duke of Normandy, 'Conqueror'	13, 17	
William, King and Mary, Queen	70	
William, son of Baldwin	19	
Wilson, Richard	73	
Winkleigh, William de	37	
Witchcraft	56, 65	
Women's Land Army	119-120	
Wood, John	56	
Wood, T.F., Manure Factory	95	
Wool (see also cloth industry)	42-43, 69, 71, 83, 126	
Woollcombe, Squire John Morth	81	
Worden, Eustace	127	
Workhouse, Okehampton Union	88, 90-91, 117	
World War I	99, 113-115, 120	
World War II	117-118	
Wrey, Sir Bourchier	76	
Wright, W.H.K., Historian	97	
Wright's, Ironmongers	67	
Yelland	11	
Yorkshire	77	
Young, John	121	